50p

Explore Britain's CASTLES

Produced by AA Publishing

EXPLORE BRITAIN'S
CASTLES

by Elizabeth Cruwys & Beau Riffenburgh

Copy Editor: Penny Hicks

Published by AA Publishing, a trading name of Automobile Association Developments Limited, whose registered office is Norfolk House, Priestley Road, Basingstoke, Hampshire RG24 9NY. Registered Number 1878835.

A catalogue record for this book is available from the British Library.
ISBN   h/b 0 7495 1048 X
          p/b 0 7495 1094 3

Colour origination by L.C. Repro and Sons Ltd, Aldermaston.
Printed and bound by Graficromo SA, Spain

The contents of this book are believed correct at the time of printing. Nevertheless, the Publishers cannot accept responsibility for errors or omissions, or for changes in details given.

Acknowledgements: all photographs are held in the Automobile Association's own library with contributions as follows:

AA PHOTO LIBRARY with contributions from; Spine J. Beazley, 10/1 R. Moss, 11 A.Lawson, 12/3 R. Elliott, 13 S & O Matthews, 14 E. Ellington, 15 R. Surman, 16 A. Baker, 17 A. Lawson, 18, 19 P. Baker, 20 R. Moss, 21 A. Baker, 22 R. Moss, 23 A. Lawson, 25a, b D. Forss, 26 T. Teegan, 27, 28 D. Forss, 29 D. Noble, 30 W. Voysey, 31 D. Forss, 32 P. Baker, 33 D. Forss, 34 S & O Matthews, 35, 36, 37 D. Forss, 40 S & O Matthews, 41 R. Mort, 42 P.Baker, 43 W. Voysey, 44 D. Forss, 45 A. Tryner, 46 R. Surman, 47 D. Forss, 48 M. Birkitt, 49 A. Tryner, 50/1 F. Stephenson, 52 D. Forss, 53 R. Elliott, 54 M. Birkitt, 55 F. Stephenson, 56 A. Besley, 57 P. Aithie, 58/9, 59 I. Burgum, 60/1 M. Allwood-Coppin, 61 P. Aithie, 63 V. Bates, 64 C. Molyneau, 65 P. Aithie, 66 I. Burgum, 67, 68 H. Williams, 69 R. Newton, 70 P. Aithie, 71 R. Eames, 72 P. Aithie, 73 T. Timms, 74/5, 75 I. Burgum, 76 P. Aithie, 78/9 R. Newton, 79 R. Eames, 80/1, 81 T. Timms, 83 J. Gravell, 84 I. Burgum, 87, 88 M. Allwood-Coppin, 89 C. Molyneau, 90/1, 91 M. Allwood-Coppin, 92 A. Molyneau, 93 I. Burgum, 94 D. Forss, 95 J. Beazley, 96 C. Lees, 97 P. Aithie, 98 J. Morrison, 99 P. Sharpe, 100 Cameron Lees, 101 L. Whitwam, 102, 103 C. Lees, 104 J. Mottershaw, 105 J. Beazley, 106/7, 107, 108 C. Lees, 109 T. Hand, 110 J. Beazley, 111, 112 P. Baker, 113 M. Adelman, 114, 115 C. Lees, 116 E. Ellington, 117 R. Weir, 118 S & G Powater, 119 K. Paterson, 120 M. Adelman, 121 A. Baker, 122, 123 S. Day, 124 J. Carney, 125 S. Day, 126 R. Weir, 127 K. Paterson, 128 M. Taylor, 129 D. Corrance, 130 J. Henderson, 131 J. Beazley, 132, 133 A. Grierly, 134 K. Paterson, 135 M. Taylor, 136 J. Henderson, 137 E. Ellington, 138, 139 R. Weir, 140 J. Beazley, 141 K. Paterson, 142 E. Ellington, 144 D. Hardley, 145 J. Henderson, 146 R. Weir, 147 D. Corrance, 148 S. Day, 149 M. Taylor, 150 S & O Matthews, 151 K. Paterson, 152 P. Sharpe, 153 S. Day, 154/5, 155 K. Paterson, 156/7 J. Henderson, 158/9 M. Taylor, 159 J. Beazley.
MARY EVANS PICTURE LIBRARY 24 Henry VIII, 78 Edward I, crowned
EDMUND NÄGELE, F,R,P,S F/Cover Bodiam Castle,
B/Cover Eilean Donan Castle

CONTENTS

Elcho Castle, a superb example of a fortified tower house

INTRODUCTION

A castle is defined as a 'properly fortified military residence'. In medieval times, the castle was home not only to the owner and his family, but also to his retinue; it was specially designed as the centre of his military operations and to protect him from his enemies. This was a product of feudalism, whereby the lord of the castle agreed to protect his vassals and provide land, while his vassals worked the land and could be called upon for military duty.

British castles tended to come in two basic types – the fortified enclosure and the fortified tower – and sometimes a combination of both. Castles like Framlingham and Dunstanburgh comprised strong walls (with towers), forming an enclosure. This would have been filled with buildings, and, in times of danger, people living outside the castle could take refuge there. An example of a fortified tower, or 'keep', is Hedingham, a vast multi-storeyed castle with immensely thick walls.

As castles grew larger, owners realised it was impractical to try to squeeze all their worldly goods, livestock, and vassals into one tower, and so extra towers and walls were built. This was the origin of great castle complexes like the Tower of London or Dover. In the 12th century, powerful gatehouses were built into the walls to provide an additional layer of protection. In some cases, the gatehouse was even further fortified with walls and ditches, forming what is known as a 'barbican'. Such an arrangement can be seen at Goodrich, and Conwy had a barbican at each end.

The First Castles in Britain

Historians do not agree about whether there were castles in Britain before the Norman Conquest. Obviously the kings and barons of the Dark Ages must have had some kind of strongholds, but their precise structures are not known.

After William the Conqueror invaded England in 1066, he needed to consolidate what he had gained and he did this by building simple castles known as 'mottes and bailies'. The mottes were mounds of earth with flattened tops upon which wooden castles were built, sometimes surrounded by wooden pallisades or fences to form an enclosure (a bailey). Great ditches and banks called 'earthworks' were constructed to provide additional protection, and these can still be seen at Castle Rising and Castle Acre. Later, the wooden pallisades were converted to stone, at many places forming small enclosure castles called 'shell keeps', of which Restormel and Clifford's Tower in York are among the best examples.

Below, the Great Hall at Bickleigh Castle displays armour from the Civil War

Below right, while Carn Brea in Cornwall has many of the picturesque attributes of a castle, it is really a folly, and has found an unlikely new life as a restaurant

Once the Normans had established a hold in Britain, more permanent structures became necessary. Within a few years of William's invasion, building in stone rather than wood was started in castles like Chepstow, Rochester, Peveril, Colchester and, of course, the great Tower of London. Most of these early castles were simple towers, although Colchester and the Tower were – and are still – impressive for their sheer size and for the high quality of the craftsmanship.

Although Norman keeps were designed for defence and intended to dominate a defeated people, they were not all alike. The castle builders skilfully turned the unique character of each site to their advantage, and keeps were variously rectangular, circular, square, multi-sided and D-shaped. At Portchester, the splendid Norman keep was built inside the walls of an existing Roman fort. Others, like Chepstow, turned natural features such as sheer cliffs to their advantage, using the added protection they provided to one or more of the castle's flanks.

Later Castles

As methods of attacking castles became more refined, so the castles' protective measures and systems were further developed in attempts to keep the fortifications more or less impregnable. In the 12th century, castle

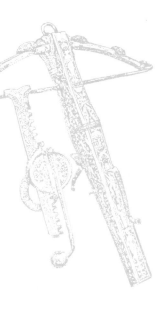

owners became aware that a simple keep, however strong and well-built, would not be able to withstand a prolonged attack. They began to build layers of defences (including 'curtain walls') around the keep in a concentric arrangement, following the example of castle builders in the Near East. The great walls of Constantinople had repelled the Crusaders, and it seems likely that the Crusaders in turn borrowed this idea from their enemies. Dover was probably the first concentric castle in Britain, followed in the late 13th century by castles such as Beaumaris and Caerphilly.

Once the Normans were firmly established in power, castle building proceeded at a more leisurely pace. At later points in history, however, it was necessary for a king to embark on a fast and furious spate of castle raising, as during the reign of Henry VIII in the 16th century. Another such occasion followed Edward I's campaigns in Wales between 1277 and 1284. The Welsh had not been idle during the previous century, and the sturdy fortresses at Ewloe and Dolbadarn are examples of Welsh-built castles. But Edward's Welsh masterpieces – magnificent, dominating structures such as Caernarfon, Conwy, Harlech and Beaumaris – were the ultimate in defensive design of any castles in Britain, and perhaps in the world. Meanwhile, in Scotland clan leaders like the Douglases were also building mighty castles, like Threave and Tantallon, while King Alexander II raised the impressive Kildrummy.

The fortified manor house began to emerge in the late 13th century, as a new kind of castle. Such houses were often surrounded by a moat, such as at

Edinburgh Castle, built high on a volcanic outcrop, dominates the city to this day

Bodiam, and although defence was still important, the comfort of the owners was also clearly taken into account. Castles were expensive to build, and only the very rich could afford to do so. While many of these fortified manor houses were small, like those at Acton Burnell or Penhow, some owners wanted their castles to be elaborately expensive in order to display their wealth and power. The magnificent brick tower at Tattershall is a splendid example of this. It was built by the Treasurer of England in the 15th century, and evidence of his riches positively oozes from the decorative stonework and luxurious chambers within.

The Castle in Scotland

Scottish castles developed several distinctive features. The Border country was subject to raids by both Scots and English for many centuries after the Scottish wars of independence were won by Robert the Bruce. In the 14th century small fortified towers, or 'peles', were built to protect local areas against these raids in northern England, while in Scotland, the distinctive 'tower-house' began to emerge. During the next 300 years, some 700 of these tower-houses were raised in Scotland, from the early ones at Drum and Crichton, to the splendid culmination of castles like Craigievar and Crathes.

Built to guard the waterways of the Carrick Roads, Pendennis Castle was one of Henry VIII's many fine coastal forts

Scottish tower-houses had thick walls, battlemented parapets and strong turrets on the corners. Many were given the additional protection of extra walls, called 'barmkins', and ditches and banks. The small doorways were often protected by iron gates called 'yetts'. After around 1500, tower-houses were provided with specially designed holes so that guns could be fired from them.

Life in a Castle

Early castles were more military garrisons than homes, but even so, their occupants had to live, and even the most desolate and inhospitable fortress was expected to have a modicum of comfort. In many rooms there were fireplaces, but since many windows would not have had glass, the stone walls and gaps at the shutters must have made them cold and gloomy places, especially in the winter. Castles would also have been noisy. The lord, his family, servants, soldiers, cooks, grooms and a host of others would have been crammed inside. Privacy was an impossible

luxury, even for the lord himself.

Many of the chambers would have had paintings, or perhaps tapestries, to decorate the walls. In most castles, there would have been rushes on the floors, although some wealthy owners might have been able to afford rugs. The heart of the castle was the hall. Meals were eaten there, and some would have used the hall as sleeping quarters after the lord had retired to bed. Later castles often had a 'solar' above the hall – an airy, pleasant room, perhaps the forerunner of the drawing room, where the lord could take his ease away from the bustle of the hall. During the daytime, the large windows would have allowed sufficient light for various household tasks to be performed, like sewing and mending. It is likely that the lord of Tolquhon used his solar to display his fine collection of books.

The Castle Under Attack

It was not easy for attackers to overpower great medieval fortresses designed to repel invaders. Most attackers therefore opted for a siege – a

Fyvie Castle, dating from the 13th century, is one of the grandest examples of Scottish baronial architecture

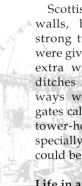

waiting game where the defences of the castle were pitted against the equipment and cunning of the attacking army. It was not unknown for treachery to be employed, as was the case when a Scottish blacksmith deliberately sabotaged Kildrummy Castle, allowing the English to take it.

Defenders might make use of the 'sally port', or back door, to harry the camp of the attackers. They could use war machines (called mangonels and trebuchets) to hurl missiles at them and, as long as supplies lasted, keep up a constant shower of arrows. These tactics were employed by Simon de Montfort the younger when he was besieged at Kenilworth in 1266.

Meanwhile, the attackers could hurl missiles back, use battering rams on the gates, or advance on the castle using the protection of 'belfries' or siege towers. If they could get close enough, attackers could undermine the walls by tunnelling underneath to weaken the foundations. A tunnel at St Andrew's was aiming to do just that when it was met with a 'countermine' dug by the castle defenders. Unable to dig further under the castle walls, the

attackers were forced to abandon their plan. King John successfully undermined one corner of Rochester's keep, with the aid of 40 dead pigs that he set alight in the tunnel. When the heat from the burning pigs caused the tunnel to collapse, part of the keep also fell, allowing John's troops in.

The Decline of the Castle

It is often said that the decline of castles came with the evolution of gunpowder, but it is more likely that the importance of castles declined because of changes in medieval society. The feudal system was no longer in place, and lords of the manor wanted comfortable residences, rather than cold and cramped fortresses. It was expensive to convert these vast medieval buildings, and it was often cheaper to build a new home. Many castles were abandoned for newer and more luxurious houses. However, some castles, like Windsor, Warwick and Glamis were never abandoned, and have been almost continuously occupied. Thus elegant palaces rub shoulders with formidable keeps, all encased within medieval curtain walls.

An example of Edwardian comfort imposed on more austere surroundings, Lindisfarne Castle

Berkeley's towers appear in martial pride,
Menacing all around the champaign wide
Right famous as the seat of barons bold
And valiant earls whose great exploits are told.
Michael Drayton (1563–1631)

BERKELEY CASTLE
Gloucestershire

BERKELEY, 10 MILES (16 KM) SOUTH-WEST OF STROUD

Serene Berkeley Castle was the scene of an appalling murder

Secluded Berkeley Castle, near the banks of the River Severn, was the site of one of the most infamous of all medieval murders. By 1327, Queen Isabella and her lover, the powerful baron Roger Mortimer, had wrested the crown from Edward II and were running the country. Edward was taken secretly to Berkeley Castle in April 1327, where attempts were made to starve him to death. Dead animals were also thrown into a pit in his room in the hope that the smell would make him sicken and die. But Edward was a strong man and Isabella saw that more drastic measures were necessary. In September, according to tradition, the unfortunate king was murdered by having a red-hot poker thrust into his bowels.

Although the chamber in which Edward is said to have been imprisoned remains, most of the castle dates from the mid 14th century and has survived essentially unchanged since then. It is a great palace-fortress built around a courtyard. Many of Berkeley's rooms are open to visitors, displaying some beautiful furnishings. One room contains furniture said to have belonged to Sir Francis Drake, while the magnificent Great Hall has a superb timber roof dating from the 14th century.

Open Easter to September, daily except Mondays, and Sunday afternoons in October. Tel: 01453 810332.

DARTMOUTH CASTLE
Devon

DARTMOUTH, 13 MILES (21 KM) SOUTH OF TORQUAY

*A*t the mouth of the River Dart a rocky promontory juts out towards the sea, and on this rock stands Dartmouth Castle – an intriguing collection of military buildings spanning six centuries. The most recent addition is a brick gun-shelter built during World War II in anticipation of a German invasion.

A castle was built at Dartmouth in the 14th century, although it was not until the 15th century that the citizens of Dartmouth really began to build their fortress in earnest. It comprised a square tower and a round tower, side by side, moulded to suit the shape of the rock, and is the earliest surviving English coastal castle designed specially for artillery. At the same time, another castle was built opposite Dartmouth at Kingswear, ensuring that no French pirates would be able to penetrate up river to pillage the wealthy town.

The castle itself saw action in the Civil War, when the town was attacked by Cromwell's forces under Sir Thomas Fairfax. In a blaze of gunfire, Fairfax's men stormed the town, taking it within hours and with remarkably few casualties. The 500 Royalists, who had captured Dartmouth Castle after a siege three years before, surrendered their arms on the following day.

Open daily from April to October; closed Monday and Tuesday in winter. Tel: 01803 833588.

CORFE CASTLE
Dorset

CORFE CASTLE, 6 MILES (10 KM) SOUTH-EAST OF WAREHAM

*O*nce regarded as one of the finest castles in England, Corfe was reduced during the Civil War to the collection of ragged walls and shattered towers that loom over the small town like broken teeth. After Cromwell's troops had captured this mighty fortress, it was subjected to an unusually brutal 'slighting' that involved undermining anything which could not be blown up with gunpowder. Perhaps this ferocity resulted from the fact that during the first siege of Corfe, the attackers were soundly repelled by Royalist troops under the command of one Lady Bankes. She undertook the defence of the castle in 1643 during her husband's absence, and not only withstood the 500 Parliamentarians and their vast array of weapons and siege equipment, but forced them to retreat leaving 100 of their comrades dead.

The second siege occurred in 1646, conveniently timed when the formidable Lady Bankes was away, but the spirited defenders held out again until eventually the siege was

Below and right, Corfe Castle has remained in its ruinous state since its destruction in the 17th century

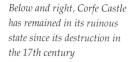

broken by an act of treachery, rather than military prowess. A small group of soldiers purporting to be Royalists were welcomed into the castle as much-needed additional manpower, but the soldiers were, in fact, Cromwell's men and they hastened to open the gates and allow the besiegers in. As soon as Cromwell's forces had taken the last prisoner, orders were given to destroy the castle so that it would never again withstand a siege.

Building first commenced on Corfe in the 1080s, on a natural hill commanding fine views of the surrounding countryside, and several kings contributed to its stone construction. Most notably, King John paid £1400 for walls, a deep ditch-and-bank defence and his 'gloriette'. Corfe was John's favourite castle and the gloriette was an unfortified residential block containing lavish accommodation for the king, a chapel and offices. Henry III and Edward I added more towers and walls, making Corfe one of the strongest and most powerful castles in the country.

Corfe Castle was particularly important to King John – he imprisoned his wife here and, four years later, he used it as a hiding place for his treasure and crown. He also used it as a prison, and 22 French knights were starved to death within its walls. Other notable prisoners kept at Corfe included Robert of Normandy, William the Conqueror's eldest son, who was kept captive for most of his life by his youngest brother, Henry I. Edward II was also imprisoned here before his fateful journey to Berkeley.

Open daily from February to October, weekend afternoons only in winter. Tel: 01929 481294.

Launceston Castle was an important military fortress in its time

※
LAUNCESTON CASTLE
Cornwall

LAUNCESTON, 23 MILES (37 KM) NORTH-WEST OF PLYMOUTH

※

King Henry III had a younger brother named Richard. It was, perhaps, an unfortunate twist of fate that made Henry the older of the two boys, for Richard was a skilful politician, a cunning diplomat and was wiser by far than his brother the King. Richard used his considerable talents to make himself one of the richest barons in the country – amassing far more wealth than Henry had ever possessed – and with his wealth came a different sort of power. He was elected King of the Romans, and even tried to secure himself the position of Holy Roman Emperor. In 1227, Richard was made Earl of Cornwall, and it was he who built the fine castle at Launceston.

Launceston is a good example of what is known as a shell keep, which consists of a circular wall with buildings inside. Inside this outer wall Richard built another tower, roofed over the space between the two walls, and added a fighting platform around the outside of the outer wall. After Richard's death in 1272, Launceston declined in importance as a military fortress, and by 1353 it was reported that pigs were endangering its foundations by trampling the moat. Launceston was also used as a prison, and it is believed that George Fox, the founder of the Quakers, was held here for eight months in 1656.

Open from April to October daily. Tel: 01566 772365.

NUNNEY CASTLE
Somerset

NUNNEY, 3 MILES (5 KM) SOUTH-WEST OF FROME

*I*n 1645 Cromwell's men set up a cannon on high ground near Nunney, preparing to lay siege to a castle which was at the time held for Charles I. Almost immediately, a hole was made in the north wall, just above the entrance, and Cromwell's troops continued firing to widen the breach. Two days later the castle garrison surrendered and the Parliamentarian soldiers swarmed into Nunney, looting and removing everything of value. The damaged wall remained standing until 1910, when it collapsed into the moat, blocking it up. The moat was later cleared, and is fed today by the small stream that runs through this pretty Somerset village.

Nunney was built by Sir John Delamere in 1373. By this time, the church had already been built in the best position in the village, and so the castle is sited on a stretch of land that most castle-builders would have rejected as too low. But Delamere was perhaps not so much interested in building a strongly defensible fortress as a splendid palace that would reflect his own rising glory (he later became Sheriff of Somerset and a Knight of the Shire). It is a roughly oblong building, with round towers at each corner, more reminiscent of a French château than an English castle, and is an attractive feature of a delightful village.

Open access at any reasonable time. Tel: 0171 973 3000.

Supposedly modelled on the Bastille, Nunney Castle has one of the deepest moats in England

Okehampton Castle stands on the northern fringe of Dartmoor National Park

OKEHAMPTON CASTLE
Devon

OKEHAMPTON, 24 MILES (38 KM) EAST OF EXETER

Set among richly wooded hills in the rolling Devon countryside, the size and strength of Okehampton Castle come as something of a surprise. Okehampton's history was relatively uneventful, and the only episode of national significance that occurred here was when one of its owners, Henry, Marquis of Exeter, was executed by Henry VIII for conspiracy in 1539, after which the castle was seized by the Crown and dismantled.

Okehampton Castle is, in fact, one of the largest and most extensive castle ruins in the West Country, and is sadly neglected by tourists. It started as a simple mound, probably before 1070, and a stone keep was erected in the late 11th century. In the early 14th century a second building was added to the keep, with thick walls and fine round-arched windows. At the same time, other buildings were raised below the keep, producing an elongated enclosure protected by walls and steep slopes. These other buildings included kitchens, more accommodation, a solar and hall, guardrooms and a chapel. A gatehouse was also raised, connected to the rest of the castle by a long, narrow tunnel. Many of the buildings are in an excellent state of preservation, and this negected castle is well worth a visit.

Open from April to October daily. Tel: 01837 52844.

ST MAWES CASTLE
Cornwall

ST MAWES, 11 MILES (17.5 KM) SOUTH OF TRURO

'We are in a very wild place, where no human being ever visits, in the midst of a most barbarous race.' So wrote an ambassador from Venice in 1506, when his ship was forced to take refuge from a violent storm in the River Fal.

In the 16th century Cornwall was indeed an isolated place, a long way from the seat of government and affairs of state, but by the 1530s, Henry VIII was on the brink of a war with France and Spain because he had divorced his Catholic wife, Catherine of Aragon. It became necessary to fortify England's south coast against a possible invasion, and the River Fal was given two forts to protect it – Pendennis on the west bank and St Mawes on the east.

St Mawes stands on a low headland on the Roseland Peninsula. Its main building is the keep, shaped like a clover leaf, which was raised between 1540 and 1545, and a great deal of care went into its building. It has more decorative carvings than any of Henry VIII's other coastal forts and was built of good quality stone. The entire fort is well-garnished with openings for cannon and other artillery, and further cannon were located outside the keep, aimed across the river.

Open daily from April to October, but closed Monday and Tuesday in winter. Tel: 01326 270526.

St Mawes Castle guards the mouth of the Fal estuary

Henry VIII and the Coastal Defence of England

Below, a portrait of the youthful King Henry VIII, and right, his coastal defences at Dover (above) and Deal

*A*lthough England and France were often at war during the Middle Ages, and despite the possibility of a French invasion, there was no systematic building of defensive sites along the south coast. Dover Castle loomed over the narrowest point of the Channel, and Southampton and the Cinque Ports were relatively secure, but towns like Dartmouth had to ask several times before a royal licence was granted to build a castle, which was to protect them against raiding pirates in the 14th century. Small gun-houses were built around Dorset, Devon and Cornwall, but nothing was built on a major scale until Henry VIII annulled his marriage to Catherine of Aragon in 1533.

Since divorce was unacceptable within the Catholic Church, Henry declared that the Church of England and Wales was no longer under Papal authority. France and Spain rallied to the Pope's outraged entreaties, and the King began to fortify his coasts against an invasion. Henry's intention was ambitious – to have some kind of military structure at every landing place from Hull, right round the coast to Milford Haven in Wales. Although this could not be achieved, Henry succeeded in building fortresses at Deal, Walmer, Sandgate, Camber, Southsea, Hurst, Sandown, Calshot, Portland, St Mawes and Pendennis. There were also smaller forts, or 'blockhouses', at ports such as Harwich, Gravesend and Brownsea. All of these were built before the mid 1540s, but the first were called 'the three castles which keep the Downs' – Deal, Walmer and Sandgate. The largest is Deal, a vast sprawling mass of thick stone walls forming six bastions grouped around a single tower. Walmer is smaller and had four, rather than six, bastions. Sandgate survived until the 19th century, but finally gave in to the assault of the sea, a victim of changing tidal patterns and salt erosion.

These forts were not castles in the strict sense of the word. They were fortified, without a doubt, but they were not homes, and soldiers were garrisoned there for a term of service rather than as a permanent residence. Because the forts had to be built quickly, local supplies were used, and the recently dissolved monasteries provided sources of stone as well as money to pay the many workers required. However, the press-ganged workers were apparently unhappy with their meagre pay. Those at Deal went on strike in 1539, but their masters were unsympathetic and the ringleaders were promptly imprisoned.

After all Henry's urgency and expense, the expected attack from France and Spain never came. Perhaps the knowledge that these formidable gun-laden castles were waiting lessened the enthusiasm of his opponents, so Henry's forts served their purpose as a deterrent rather than a defence.

The Cinque Ports – Dover, Hastings, Hythe, Romney and Sandwich – belonged to an economic alliance of coastal towns dating back to the 11th century. These important medieval trading points were, by royal command, heavily fortified with walls and towers. Because of the extensive silting of its estuary, Sandwich is no longer on the coast.

TINTAGEL CASTLE
Cornwall

TINTAGEL, 2 MILES (3 KM) NORTH OF CAMELFORD

*I*n the winter, ferocious storms whip up around the rugged Cornish coast, wearing away at the rocky peninsula that is home to the scanty remains of Tintagel Castle. Each year parts are swept away, and so what remains today is not what would have existed when Reginald, an illegitimate son of Henry I, first raised his castle here.

Tintagel is traditionally associated with the legend of King Arthur, who, it is said, was conceived here while Merlin waited in a cave under the castle. The cave that pierces the thin neck of rock which joins the peninsula to the mainland is still called Merlin's Cave, and it can be visited at low tide. This is a wild and desolate place,

Subjected to erosion by the sea, Tintagel Castle is a dramatic sight

where it is easy to imagine the romantic image of the legendary hero, but there is no concrete evidence to support the connection.

About 100 years after Reginald had built his square hall, Richard, Earl of Cornwall, built two more enclosures and raised some walls. The Black Prince built another hall, and there is evidence that yet another was raised over the remains of the previous two. Archaeologically, Tintagel is difficult to understand, and there are foundations of buildings and several tunnels, the purpose of which remains unknown – all adding to the castle's air of mystery.

Open all year, except at Christmas and New Year. Tel: 01840 770328.

ALLINGTON CASTLE
Kent

2 MILES (3 KM) NORTH-WEST OF MAIDSTONE

In the early years of the 20th century, Allington was restored by the British traveller Sir Martin Conway, who was particularly well known for his adventures and explorations in the Arctic.

The medieval castle at Allington, on the banks of the Medway just outside Maidstone, has had an eventful history that converted it from a 13th-century fortress to a grand Tudor mansion, a farmhouse, a stately home and finally a convent for Carmelite nuns.

The first castle on this site was raised in the 11th century, and was probably only a simple mound with a wooden structure on the top. A stone castle was built by Stephen of Penchester, under a licence granted by Edward I in 1281. (For fear lest his barons became too powerful, no one was allowed to build without royal permission.)

The oldest part of the early stone castle to survive is a section of wall that displays a distinctive herringbone pattern, made by laying the stones in zig-zags. The castle was converted into a mansion in the 15th century, but there was a serious fire in about 1600, leaving only enough of the mansion to make a farmhouse. Substantial restoration work was carried out before the castle was taken over by the Carmelite order in 1951.

Privately owned, the castle is not open to the public except for occasional special events. Contact the Tourist Office, Maidstone, tel: 01622 602169, for information.

Allington Castle, bypassed by battles and sieges, has been shaped by more peaceful events

Still a family home, Arundel reflects the changes of nearly a thousand years

ARUNDEL CASTLE
Sussex

ARUNDEL, 12 MILES (19 KM) EAST OF CHICHESTER

The charming palace-castle which sprawls among the trees in this attractive West Sussex town has so many battlemented towers and chimneys that it has an almost fairy-tale appearance. There has been a castle at Arundel for some 900 years, ever since a castle mound was raised in about 1088. Around 100 years later, a circular shell keep was built on the mound and at the same time, or perhaps a little later, walls, a chapel and a garden were added by Henry II. It is possible that this was the first royal garden in England.

Most of the castle, however, is more recent, and owes much to the work of the 11th Duke of Norfolk, who, in 1787, began to renovate and reconstruct Arundel so that it could become his main home outside London. Subsequent Dukes have continued this work, and today there are many splendid rooms packed with treasures on view to the public. The collection of paintings is especially fine, containing works by such artists as Van Dyck, Lely, Reynolds, Lawrence and Gainsborough.

In the chapel, marble columns soar upwards to gothic arches and an intriguing striped ceiling, and many of the state rooms contain exquisite furnishings.

Open from April to October, daily except Sunday. Tel: 01903 883136.

BODIAM CASTLE
East Sussex

12 MILES (19 KM) NORTH OF HASTINGS

With its battlemented walls and towers reflected in a moat dotted with water-lilies, Bodiam is one of the most picturesque castles in Britain. But beauty was hardly the prime objective of Bodiam's builder when he constructed his castle and dug his moat – this was a fortress designed to repel invaders and to provide a haven of safety for those lucky enough to be secure within its walls.

Bodiam was built by Sir Edward Dalyngrygge between 1385 and 1388. Richard II had granted him a licence to fortify his manor house after the nearby port of Rye had been attacked by the French. Interpreting the licence somewhat more liberally than had been intended, Dalyngrygge promptly abandoned his old manor house and set about building Bodiam Castle.

The castle is rectangular, with a round tower at each corner and a square tower midway along each wall; two of these square towers form gateways. Bodiam is totally surrounded by the wide moat, across which a series of bridges originally gave access to the castle, some at right angles to each other to prevent storming. These elaborate defences against attack were never seriously tested – Bodiam was involved in a skirmish in 1484, but during the Civil War it was surrendered without a shot being fired.

Open all year, except Mondays between November and March, and Christmas. Tel: 01580 830436.

Bodiam Castle remains relatively intact today, proof of its peaceful past

CARISBROOKE CASTLE
Isle of Wight

CARISBROOKE, JUST SOUTH-WEST OF NEWPORT

While a prisoner in Carisbrooke Castle in the summer of 1647, Charles I claimed to his startled supporters that he could escape from his prison because he had tested the size of the bars on the window against his head. What his head could pass through, the rest of his body, he assured his friends, could follow. After some undignified struggling, Charles was forced to admit that he had misjudged. Unfortunately for Charles, this was not his only error of judgement, and he was executed in London some 18 months later.

A mound was built here in about 1070, four years after the Battle of Hastings, and a stone shell keep was built on the mound 70 years later. In the 14th century, England feared an attack by the French, and it was at this time that the spectacular gatehouse was built. The French did actually manage to land on the island, but the castle was not attacked.

In the 1580s, it was the Spanish who threatened invasion, and the castle was altered and adapted so that it would be able to repel an attack by guns. There are several buildings in the castle courtyard, one of which houses a museum, another the well house.

Open all year daily, except at Christmas and New Year. Tel: 01983 522107.

Carisbrooke is the island's only remaining medieval castle

Deal Castle, where Iron Age weapons and relics of Deal's history are displayed

---
※
DEAL CASTLE
Kent

DEAL, 9 MILES (14.5 KM) NORTH-EAST OF DOVER
※
---

*I*n 1533 Henry VIII, disappointed at not having produced a healthy son, divorced his Catholic wife, Catherine of Aragon. This move resulted not only in Henry being excommunicated, but also brought him in direct conflict with Catholic France and Spain. In order to protect England's southern coasts, Henry built a series of forts, financed largely from the proceeds of the dissolved monasteries.

Deal and nearby Walmer are two of these forts, both plain, functional buildings, where the sole purpose was defence. At Deal, six semi-circular bastions are joined to form a tower, which is further protected by an outer wall of the same shape. All were liberally supplied with gun loops and cannon ports, so that, in all, an attacker faced five tiers of guns. Walmer has a simpler plan, involving a circular tower and a quatrefoil outer wall, but the defensive principle is the same, and from every angle an invader would face a bristling armoury of handguns and cannon.

As it happened, Henry's precautions were not necessary and Deal was not attacked until 1648, when it was held for Charles I in the Civil War. It suffered extensive damage, but was not attacked again until a bomb fell on it during World War II.

Open all year, but closed on Monday and Tuesday between November and March. Tel: 01304 372762.

The Cinque Ports
Walmer is the official residence of the Lords Warden of the Cinque Ports, a commercial alliance of south coast ports dating from the 11th century. Winston Churchill held this office between 1941 and 1965, and the present holder is HM Queen Elizabeth The Queen Mother.

DOVER CASTLE
Kent

DOVER, 7 MILES (11.5 KM) EAST OF FOLKESTONE

Within the castle grounds are a Roman lighthouse and a beautiful little Anglo-Saxon church.

Below, rich in history, Dover Castle was used during World War II to plan the evacuation of Dunkirk

Below right, the Saxon church of St Mary de Castros

Dover Castle is so enormous, and contains so many fascinating features, that it is difficult to know where to start in its description. It was a state-of-the-art castle in medieval times, displaying some of the most highly advanced defensive architecture available. Its strategically vital position at the point where England is nearest to the coast of France has given it a unique place in British history. And it is simultaneously powerful, massive, imposing and splendid.

The castle stands on a spur of rock overlooking the English Channel. The entire site is protected by walls bristling with towers and bulwarks. These include the formidable Constable's Gate, erected in the 1220s, a pair of D-shaped towers that not only served as a serious obstacle for would-be invaders, but provided comfortable lodgings for the castle constables (or, nowadays, their deputies). Outside the walls are earthworks and natural slopes that provide additional defence.

The castle was begun by William the Conqueror, but the great keep was built by Henry II in the 1180s. It is surrounded by yet another wall, studded with square towers and two barbicans. The keep itself is 95 feet (29m) tall, and around 95 feet (29m) across at its base. There are square turrets at each corner, and even at the top of the tower, where the walls are thinnest, they are still 17 feet (5.2m) thick. The well is carved into the thickness of the wall, and plunges 240 feet (73m) to reach a steady water supply.

Dover has had a rich and eventful history, and one especially important episode occurred during the last year of the reign of King John (1216). John's barons had been growing increasingly frustrated with him, and had invited Prince Louis, heir to the French throne, to invade England and take over. Louis landed at Dover and laid siege to Dover Castle, which was held by Hubert de Burgh, a baron loyal to John. Ever since the castle was founded, kings had laid down vast sums of money for its repair and development (notably Henry II and Richard I), and it looked as though this investment had paid off. Louis, it seemed, would be unable to breach Dover's powerful walls. Then the unthinkable happened – the French managed to take the outer barbican and undermine the gate. Despite de Burgh's efforts, Louis was poised to enter the inner enclosure. With fortunate timing, John died, the barons proclaimed allegiance to his successor, Henry III, and Louis went home. Lessons were learned, however, and Henry spent a good deal of money in improving Dover's defences.

Open all year daily, except Christmas and New Year. Tel: 01304 823292.

Herstmonceux, one of the most striking 15th-century castles in Britain

HERSTMONCEUX CASTLE
East Sussex

8 MILES (13 KM) NORTH OF EASTBOURNE

Many people will associate the fine brick palace at Herstmonceux with the Royal Observatory, which moved here from Greenwich in 1948. In 1989 the Royal Observatory moved yet again, leaving Herstmonceux to adjust to its new existence as a conference centre. It was one of the first castles in England to be built of brick, and the effect is stunning. Its clusters of elegant chimneys and the many towers, all in a pleasing shade of rich red, are reflected in the wide moat that surrounds it, rendering it one of the most attractive castles built in the Middle Ages.

Sir Roger Fiennes was granted a licence to build Herstmonceux in 1441.

The fact that the castle was built in a lake afforded some protection, and the impressive gatehouse presented a formidable array of murder holes and arrow slits with which to greet hostile visitors.

Once the castle had passed from the Fiennes family, it had a sad history of careless owners. In the 17th century, one owner shamelessly ripped the interior of the castle out in order to provide himself with the raw materials to build another house, and a great deal of work has been necessary to restore it to its former grandeur.

The castle is not open to the public, but the grounds are open at certain times of year. Tel: 0323 833913.

LEEDS CASTLE
Kent

5 MILES (8 KM) EAST OF MAIDSTONE

*L*eeds Castle is not, as many would-be visitors might suppose, in the city of Leeds in West Yorkshire, but in the depths of the beautiful Kent countryside. It takes its name from its first owner, a man named Leed, or Ledian, who built himself a wooden castle in 857. Leed was the Chief Minister of the King of Kent, and in a time where a fall from grace or an attack by rival parties was a way of life, Leed was very wise in building a stronghold for his family on the two small islands in the lake formed by the River Len.

It is difficult to imagine what the original Leeds Castle must have looked like, especially when confronted by the grandeur of the building that stands on the two islands today. Edward I rebuilt the earlier Norman castle, providing it with a set of outer walls, a barbican, and the curious 'gloriette', a D-shaped tower on the smaller of the two islands, which was altered extensively in the Tudor period. Much of Leeds Castle was restored and rebuilt in the 19th century, and many of the rooms are open to the public, all lavishly decorated, with superb collections of art and furniture.

Open daily April to October, weekends only in winter. Tel: 01622 765400.

Leeds Castle has, in one of its out-buildings, a most unusual museum dedicated to medieval dog collars.

Leeds Castle, set in 500 acres of landscaped parkland, has been beautifully restored

Pevensey Castle, although threatened on occasions, has never been taken by force

PEVENSEY CASTLE
East Sussex

4 MILES (6 KM) NORTH-EAST OF EASTBOURNE

At nine o'clock in the morning of Thursday, 28 September 1066, an invading army landed on the English coast. Their leader, William, Duke of Normandy, a veteran of many battles, immediately seized the Roman fort at Pevensey and dug ditches to provide his troops with added protection in the event of an attack. The attack did not come, and William quickly moved his army to a better site along the coast at Hastings, where he erected his first castle.

Once the Battle of Hastings was over, and Duke William became King William, the Normans needed to consolidate their position by building castles and controlling the land around them. William gave Pevensey to his half-brother, Robert of Mortain, who built a castle inside the old Roman fort. Years later, perhaps about 1100, work started on raising a large keep.

The castle has had many owners, and has been besieged on several occasions, notably by William II in 1088, Stephen of Penchester in 1147, and Simon de Montfort the Younger in 1264–1265. The last siege is perhaps the most famous. It happened after the Battle of Lewes, in which Henry III was defeated by his barons. The King's supporters took refuge in the town of Pevensey, but Simon de Montfort was unable to take the castle.

Open all year, but closed Monday and Tuesday from November to March. Tel: 01323 762604.

PORTCHESTER CASTLE
Hampshire

4 MILES (6 KM) EAST OF FAREHAM

The origins of Portchester castle stretch much further back in time than its Norman buildings, for Portchester was a Roman coastal fortress constructed in the 3rd century AD. The Roman walls still stand tall and strong today, as they did when the Normans came and built a great keep inside this sturdy fortress.

The Roman fort was a great square enclosure, protected by high walls studded with protective towers. In 1120 the Normans built a fine keep using cut stone imported from Caen in France. Originally the keep was only two storeys high, but about 50 years later it was given an additional two floors, and 200 years after this, Richard II added battlements.

Because of its strategically important position on the coast, several medieval kings spent a good deal of money on maintaining and improving the castle. Richard II is believed to have raised the buildings between the keep and the gatehouse called 'Richard's Palace'. Edward I presented the castle first to his mother and then to his wife. Before the castle came into royal hands, Augustinian Canons built a priory in the south-eastern corner of the fort, and their splendid chapel can still be seen by visitors to the castle.

Open all year daily, except Christmas and New Year. Tel: 01705 378291.

Left to fall into disrepair, only parts of Portchester Castle remain today

The Mottes of William the Conqueror

When William landed at Pevensey with his Norman army in September 1066 to claim the English throne, he was faced with a Roman fortress. Ever quick to seize upon an advantage, William took the fort and strengthened it with ditches. Still unchallenged, he quickly moved his army to the better site at Hastings, to prepare himself for his coming battle with his rival for the English throne, King Harold.

The Bayeux Tapestry shows William pressing local people to build him a 'motte' – a cone of earth – on top of which he raised a wooden fort. It seems likely that William actually brought this fort with him, in the form of ready-cut pieces of wood and barrels of nuts and bolts. The simple wooden structure at Hastings was the first of several hundred castles built by the Normans during the next hundred years. Records suggest that William raised almost 100 mottes all over England, while his son, William II, added another hundred,

including several in Wales. Mottes were usually built on existing higher ground, but sometimes had to be raised from scratch. A great variety of materials were used, and sometimes the mottes were enormous – the one at Thetford was 80 feet (24m) tall, with a formidable array of banks and ditches to help protect it.

Motte and bailey castles were simple in structure, and usually conformed to a basic plan. The motte was raised first, perhaps taking a gang of a hundred labourers two or three weeks; the top was then flattened and a palisade of wooden stakes would be hammered in around the edges. A high wooden tower was built in the middle of the palisade, forming a watch-tower over the surrounding countryside, and this was the last line of defence against a siege. Below the motte, a further enclosure was sealed off with stakes, forming the bailey. Later, wood was replaced with stone. Attacking one of these mottes would have been no simple matter. The sides are invariably steep and would probably have been

The Bayeux Tapestry gives a delightful picture of William's first motte and fort at Hastings

William went on to claim the rest of England, building further castles as he went

slippery, and any attacker climbing to the summit would have been an easy target for the archers that would have been stationed all around the top.

Numerous mottes can still be seen in Britain. Some are crowned with shell keeps, like Clifford's Tower and Totnes, while others, like Cambridge and Leicester, have long since been stripped of their stonework, and present bare grassy knolls that look out across ancient cities. Still others, such as Warwick, had their mottes incorporated into later castle complexes, while Lewes and Lincoln castles have two mottes each.

The motte at Totnes still supports a tower

Rochester Castle's well was 65 feet (20m) deep, and was constructed so that water could be drawn up from any of the keep's four floors.

ROCHESTER CASTLE
Kent

ROCHESTER, 10 MILES (16 KM) NORTH OF MAIDSTONE

The massive Norman keep of Rochester Castle

The magnificent Norman keep at Rochester has seen more than its share of battles and sieges, but perhaps the most famous one was in 1215. Shortly after the barons forced King John to sign the Magna Carta, he turned against them in a bitter war. Rochester Castle was held for the barons, and John laid siege to it with incredible ferocity. The siege lasted for about seven weeks, during which time those in the castle were reduced to a diet of horsemeat and water. Meanwhile, John kept a constant barrage of missiles from crossbows and ballistas (stone-throwing machines), and began to dig a tunnel under the keep itself. Part of the keep collapsed, but the defenders bravely fought on. Those men who could no longer fight were sent out, where it is said John had their hands and feet cut off. But Rochester finally fell, and the defenders were imprisoned.

Building on the keep started in about 1127, and it is one of the largest in England. Its walls soar to 113 feet (34m) and are up to 12 feet (3.7m) thick. Although this was first and foremost a defensive building, there are some beautifully carved archways and windows.

Open all year daily, except Christmas and New Year. Tel: 01634 402276.

WINDSOR CASTLE
Berkshire

WINDSOR, 2 MILES (3 KM) SOUTH OF SLOUGH

Windsor Castle is not only the official residence of HM The Queen, but also the largest inhabited castle in the world. The battlemented towers and turrets have been fortress, home and court to English monarchs since the 11th century.

William the Conqueror began work on the castle, raising a simple motte and bailey structure on a chalk cliff. Since then, Windsor has been almost continuously occupied, and many kings changed or added buildings during the next 900 years. Thus Henry II remodelled the great Round Tower, Edward III began to convert the military buildings into a royal residence, Edward IV started (and Henry VIII completed) the elegant St George's Chapel, and Henry VIII added the fine gatehouse. In the 1820s George IV spent a million pounds on modernising and repairing this splendid medieval fortress. The castle remained virtually unchanged from that time until the devastating fire in 1993, which destroyed parts of the historic buildings.

Windsor was a favourite among kings. Henry I was married here, Henry II planted a herb garden and regarded the castle as home, and Henry III famously entertained the local poor to a great feast here one Good Friday. Edward III was born in the castle, and his Knights of the Order of the Garter were later to adopt St George's Chapel as their place of worship. The castle withstood two sieges by King John during the Magna Carta Wars.

State apartments open all year, but subject to closure at short notice. Tel: 01753 831118.

Windsor is the largest inhabited castle in the world

The Tower is the scene of some historic ceremonies. Coronations and royal birthdays are celebrated by guns fired from the Tower, but perhaps more famous is the Ceremony of the Keys, carried out as the Tower is locked each night.

The Tower of London is one of the most outstanding examples of Norman architecture in Europe

TOWER OF LONDON
Central London

TOWER HILL, EC3

Standing proud and strong in the very heart of England's capital city, the Tower of London has had a long and eventful history. It conjours up many images for visitors – Beefeaters and ravens, the Crown Jewels, Traitors' Gate – and a multitude of executions.

William the Conqueror began work on the keep, known as the White Tower, in about 1078, but it was probably completed by William II some 20 years later. Building in the Tower of London complex has continued throughout history, right up to the Waterloo Barracks, built in 1845, and the brand new high-security jewel house. The variety of the buildings reflects the Tower's use as a royal residence, a prison, the Mint, the Royal Zoo, a public records office, the Royal Observatory and the stronghold for the crown jewels.

The Tower is noted for its bloody history. The first execution here is thought to have been that of Sir Simon Burley, who was beheaded in 1388. Two different places of execution are connected with the tower: Tower Hill, a patch of land outside the castle walls which was for public executions, and the more discreet Tower Green, inside the castle in the shadow of the White Tower. In 1465 a permanent scaffold was erected on Tower Hill by Edward IV. Countless heads followed the unfortunate Simon Burley's, including those of Sir Thomas More (1535),

Thomas Cromwell, the Earl of Essex (1540), and John Dudley, the Duke of Northumberland, and his son Guilford (1553). Tower Green witnessed the execution of two of Henry VIII's wives and the unlucky 16-year-old Lady Jane Grey, executed by 'Bloody Mary' in 1554.

Not everyone detained at the Tower was executed, and famous prisoners who languished within the gloomy walls included Princess Elizabeth (later Elizabeth I), Judge Jeffries and William Penn. But even when not under the threat of execution, prisoners were not necessarily safe. Henry VI was murdered in the Wake-field Tower in 1471, and the boy king, Edward V and his brother, the Duke of York, are believed to have been murdered in the Bloody Tower. A number of prisoners attempted an escape – some successfully, like the charismatic Ranulf Flambard, Bishop of Durham, who climbed down a rope smuggled in to him in a jug of wine. Others were less fortunate – Gruffudd, the son of Llywelyn the Great, attempted a similar escape, but the rope broke as he climbed down it and he fell to his death.

Open all year, but closed Sundays between November and February, and at Christmas. Tel: 0171-709 0765.

Tradition has it that if the ravens ever leave the Tower, the monarchy will fall. Today, precautions are taken against such an event, including clipping the ravens' wings and keeping a number of extra ravens to hand.

CASTLE ACRE
Norfolk

13 MILES (21 KM) EAST OF KING'S LYNN

*T*his modest castle lies near the great Cluniac monastery of Castle Acre Priory. A castle mound was raised here by the Earls of Surrey in about AD 1080, and the first stone castle was added in the 11th or 12th century. No visitor to the site today could fail to notice the enormous earthworks that were dug to protect it – great grassy ditches and ramparts swing around the castle, enclosing a sizeable portion of land. By looking carefully at the ground in the enclosure, you might see the regular lines and grooves in the grass which are the foundations of former castle buildings.

The archaeological explorations that have taken place already on the rectangular tower that squats on the low mound at Castle Acre have given rise to some intense debate. Some people believe that the ruined walls on the northern half of the tower may have been part of a great keep, like those at Castle Rising or Norwich, while others believe that the walls are too small to support such substantial buildings. Until further work is done, the real scale of Castle Acre's walls and buildings will remain a mystery.

Open daily April to September, and most days in winter, except Christmas and New Year. Tel: 01760 755394.

Today there are only ruins and earthworks at Castle Acre, but even these are on an impressive scale

ASHBY DE LA ZOUCH
Leicestershire

ASHBY-DE-LA-ZOUCH, 9 MILES (14.5 KM) SOUTH-EAST OF
BURTON UPON TRENT

The impressive ruins of Ashby de la Zouch include the splendid 15th-century Warwick Tower

A hall was founded at Ashby in the 12th century, but its principal feature, the keep, was not built until the 15th century. The owner, William, Lord Hastings, was granted a licence to convert the hall into a castle in 1474, at the same time as he started building his picturesque fortified house at Kirby Muxloe. Hastings' keep was about 90 feet (27m) tall and had four floors. There was also an extension on the north-east side of the tower, which had seven floors. Although there were already two wells in the castle, the keep had another of its own – a sensible precaution, for it meant that no one could tamper with the water supply.

Lord Hastings' own story shows how fortunes and the favour of kings could rise and fall in the Middle Ages. He rose to power dramatically under the Yorkist King Edward IV, becoming Lord Chamberlain as a reward for his loyalty throughout the Wars of the Roses. After Edward's death in 1483, Hastings, on the advice of Edward's mistress Jane Shore, refused to support his successor, Richard III. Richard had Hastings beheaded – a scene in history that was immortalised in Shakespeare's *Richard III*.

Open daily from April to October. Tel: 01530 413343.

COLCHESTER CASTLE
Essex

COLCHESTER, 17 MILES (27.5 KM) SOUTH OF IPSWICH

Colchester is the largest Norman keep ever to have been built in Britain – larger even than the enormous Tower of London. Its dimensions are staggering –150 feet (46m) from north to south, 110 feet (34m) from east to west and as much as 110 feet (34m) high at its corner turrets. At their splayed bases, the walls are 17 feet (5.2m) thick, but taper slightly as they rise. Because it bears some similarities to the White Tower of London, some scholars believe that both were designed by Gandulf, Bishop of Rochester.

Unfortunately, the keep lost its upper storeys in the 17th century. There were originally four floors, but in 1683, the castle was sold to one John Wheeley, who wanted to pull it down and sell the stones. The great keep proved stronger than Wheeley had anticipated, and he gave up his demolition after the top two floors had proved something of a struggle. The idea of plundering ancient buildings arouses feelings of horror in these days of heritage conservation, but the castle itself was built from stones taken from nearby Roman ruins, and stands on the foundations of the Roman Temple of Claudius.

The castle now houses a museum, including archaeological finds from Colchester – the first capital of Roman Britain.

Open all year, daily, except Christmas. Tel: 01206 712931/712932.

Colchester Castle, once known to the Saxons as King Coel's Palace, after the Old King Cole of the nursery rhyme

FRAMLINGHAM CASTLE
Suffolk

FRAMLINGHAM, 18 MILES (29 KM) NORTH OF IPSWICH

*The magnificent curtain
walls of Framlingham Castle*

The battlemented towers and walls of Framlingham Castle have had some notable owners. The castle that survives today was probably built by the powerful Earl of Norfolk, Roger Bigod, between about 1189 and 1200 on the site of an earlier castle. The Bigods traditionally had tempestuous relationships with their kings – Hugh Bigod supported Henry II's eldest son when he rebelled against his father in 1173, Roger Bigod II held Framlingham against King John in 1216 and Roger Bigod IV refused to go to Flanders to fight for Edward I in 1297.

Framlingham was also owned by the Mowbray family, one of whom was engaged to marry one of the unfortunate princes who disappeared in the Tower of London. It was at Framlingham that 'Bloody' Mary learned that she had become Queen of England in 1553. Later, Queen Elizabeth I used the castle as a prison for priests who defied the new Church of England.

Framlingham has 13 towers, all connected by walls, and a wall-walk that is still open to visitors runs right round the castle. When Framlingham was no longer used as a ducal residence, it took on several different roles through the centuries, including poorhouse (the buildings for which survive in the courtyard), parish meeting place, dance hall, courtroom, drill hall and fire station.

Open all year daily, except Christmas and New Year. Tel: 01728 723330.

Hedingham, like most Norman keeps, has its main entrance on the first, rather than the ground floor. This would have been accessed by a wooden staircase that could be pulled inside the castle in times of danger.

HEDINGHAM CASTLE
Essex

CASTLE HEDINGHAM, 7 MILES (11 KM) SOUTH-WEST OF SUDBURY

When the barons forced King John to sign the Magna Carta in 1215, they doubtless thought that it would bring an end to John's unpopular policies, but John was not bowed for long. Robert de Vere was the owner of Hedingham Castle, and among other of the barons who sided against their king, had his castle attacked twice in what became known as the Magna Carta Wars. John died soon afterwards, and Hedingham and other properties were restored to de Vere, whose family continued to own the castle until 1703.

Today, only the keep remains of the great 12th-century fortress, but it is one of the finest in England. The exact date that it was raised is not certain, but it was probably sometime between 1120 and 1140.

It has four storeys, although the second floor is double the height of the others. This second floor forms a magnificent hall, with elegant arched windows on two levels to provide plenty of light. The whole room is spanned by a vast Norman arch, and a gallery runs around the upper half of this splendid chamber.

Open from Easter to October, daily. Tel: 01787 60261.

The great keep of Hedingham Castle is one of the best preserved in Europe

Lincoln Castle is a popular spot for 'living history' events

※
LINCOLN CASTLE
Lincolnshire

LINCOLN, 16 MILES (26 KM) NORTH-EAST OF NEWARK-ON-TRENT
※
---

*I*n 1068 William the Conqueror ordered that a castle should be built in Lincoln on a site that had been occupied since Roman times, and 166 houses were cleared away in order to make room for it. It seems inconceivable today that so many people could be uprooted from their homes at a moment's notice, but such cavalier actions on the part of landowners were not uncommon in medieval times, and the historical records of many castles tell of such clearances.

Lincoln is one of the very few castles in Britain that has two 'mottes' or castle mounds (Lewes in East Sussex is another). The larger of these two mottes has a 15-sided keep called the Lucy Tower, named after the mother of a 12th-century owner, Lucy, Countess of Chester. The smaller motte has a square tower with a 19th-century observatory, and huge 12th-century walls join the two mottes and enclose an area of about five acres (2ha).

Until recently, Lincoln housed a prison, and one of the most interesting features is the prison chapel, designed as a series of small cubicles so that the prisoners could not see each other.

Open all year daily, except Sundays and Christmas Day. Tel: 01522 511068.

Sir Walter Scott's novel
Kenilworth was published in
1821. It tells of events that
were supposed to have
occurred during the visit of
Elizabeth I to the castle
in 1575.

KENILWORTH CASTLE
Warwickshire

KENILWORTH, 5 MILES (8 KM) SOUTH-WEST OF COVENTRY

*T*he deep red stones of one of Britain's mightiest keeps was the scene of one of the most important sieges in English history. In 1238 a young French noble, who had claimed a tenuous hold on the earldom of Leicester, secretly married King Henry III's recently widowed sister. The young noble was Simon de Montfort, and during the next 27 years he would become one of Henry's greatest friends and most bitter enemies. Henry gave Kenilworth to his brother-in-law in 1244, but later de Montfort voiced his opposition to the absolute power of the monarchy and openly declared war on the king, making Kenilworth his rebel headquarters. At first, many nobles were struck by the sense of de Montfort's proposals, and they flocked to his cause. Even Henry's son Edward, heir to the throne of England, took de Montfort's side against his father at first. When he eventually changed sides, de Montfort imprisoned him at Kenilworth Castle. Edward escaped and played a vital

role in the defeat and death of de Montfort at the Battle of Lewes in 1265.

De Montfort's supporters fled to Kenilworth, where the rebellion continued under his son. The siege that was to follow lasted six months, and was perhaps one of the most violent ever to take place on English soil. Because the castle was protected on three sides by water, the attackers could not undermine the walls and had to concentrate instead on trying to breach the great defences of the gatehouse and walls. Contemporary accounts tell how besiegers and besieged hurled missiles at each other from great war machines. So intense was this fire, that the stones exploded as they crashed into each other in mid-air. The castle was finally overcome by starvation, not because the castle could no longer be defended.

The first castle at Kenilworth was a simple mound with wooden buildings, and the magnificent keep was not raised until the 12th century. It was a massive building, with an entrance on the first floor that was protected by a substantial forebuilding. Robert Dudley, Earl of Leicester, was responsible for changing the narrow windows into large ones that would flood the upper chambers with light. Dudley was the favourite of Elizabeth I, and he lived in constant expectation of a visit from her. He built a fine gatehouse and a graceful residential suite, intended specifically for the Queen.

Much has survived of this important castle. The great red keep looms powerfully over the elegant 16th-century residences, all still protected by strong walls, earthworks and the great mere.

Open all year daily, except Christmas and New Year. Tel: 01926 52078.

Below, although Cromwell ordered Kenilworth to be demolished, enough remains today to show what a magnificent fortress it must have been

Orford Castle was built with the dual objects of protecting the coast and keeping an eye on the Bigod family

---
❊

ORFORD CASTLE
Suffolk

ORFORD, 12 MILES (19 KM) EAST OF WOODBRIDGE

❊

When Henry II came to the throne in 1154, it was quickly apparent that he had not inherited a trouble-free kingdom from King Stephen. The barons had manipulated the strife between Stephen and his rival for the throne, Matilda (Henry's mother), to accrue personal power. One such baron was Hugh Bigod, Earl of Norfolk, who owned many of the castles in the East Anglian region. Henry II knew that in order to control the land, he must first control the castles. He took several castles that belonged to Bigod, and set about building one of his own at Orford in 1165.

Orford Castle was completed in two years, and comprised an unusual keep surrounded by walls and defensive towers. Today, only the keep survives, but it is one of the most remarkable keeps in England. It is 21-sided on the outside, and round on the inside, rises to some 90 feet (27 m) in height and has five storeys with small chambers in the walls.

It has been well preserved, and its rooms offer a real sensation of what life would have been like in a medieval castle. Standing outside, looking up at its great creamy-grey walls, it is also easy to appreciate the size and strength of this formidable tower.

Open all year daily, except Christmas and New Year. Tel: 01394 450472.

CASTLE RISING CASTLE
Norfolk

CASTLE RISING, 5½ MILES (9 KM) NORTH-EAST OF KING'S LYNN

In the castle grounds there are the remains of an 11th-century chapel. Their position, half covered by earthworks, suggest that the chapel was destroyed in order to make way for the castle.

*I*n 1327 the unfortunate King Edward II was horribly murdered in Berkeley Castle on the orders of his wife, Queen Isabella, and her lover, Roger Mortimer. At this time, Edward's heir, Edward III, was only 15 years old, and Mortimer and Isabella were able to rule England together by manipulating the young King. This state of affairs continued for three years until Edward III began to take matters back into his own hands. Learning of the roles of his mother and Mortimer in the death of his father, Edward had Mortimer tried for treason and hanged in 1330. Isabella, as guilty as Mortimer, was spared trial and execution, but was banished from the court. She spent the last 30 years or so of her life at Castle Rising, joining an order of nuns called the Poor Clares in her old age.

Although it is easy to look at the strong walls of the mighty keep at Castle Rising and imagine the fallen Queen confined, lonely and forgotten in her castle prison, there is no evidence that she was physically constrained there. In fact, there is some suggestion that she regularly toured around the area. It is more likely that Isabella's long sojourn at Castle Rising was her own choice, and that living out her days in the quiet peace of Norfolk was her penance for her part in the brutal murder of her husband.

There are many fascinating points about Castle Rising. As late as the 18th century, paintings of the castle show ships in the background, for when the castle was built in the 12th century it was near the sea, or at least accessible from the sea. No visitor to Castle Rising can fail to notice the massive Norman earthworks that surround the castle. Great ditches and mounds were thrown up, with walls added later, and still today – even without the threat of archers sending out hails of arrows – the grassy earthworks are difficult to scale.

The mighty, square keep was built between 1138 and 1140, although alterations to entrances and fireplaces were carried out later, and several rooms remain in excellent condition. They include a handsome wall passage and a chapel, complete with a small wall cupboard, on one of the upper floors. There is a well in the basement of the main tower and another in the castle grounds.

Open all year daily, except Christmas and New Year. Tel: 01553 631330.

The castle is famous for its connection with Edward II's queen, Isabella

TATTERSHALL CASTLE
Lincolnshire

8 MILES (13 KM) SOUTH-WEST OF HORNCASTLE

Surrounded by a moat and earth-works, the great red-brick tower of Tattershall stands proudly in the rolling Lincolnshire countryside. The tower is vast, its red-brown brick contrasting vividly with the bright white stone of its windows and 'machicolations' – projecting parapets with holes in them to permit objects to be thrown or fired at attackers.

Records show that nearly one million bricks were used to build the 100 foot (30m) high tower and associated buildings. It was constructed between 1430 and 1450 for Ralph, Lord Cromwell, who was Treasurer of England. Cromwell wanted Tattershall to be an aggressive statement of his power and authority, hence the formidable array of machicolations 80 feet (24m) above the ground, and the once extensive systems of water-filled moats and earthworks.

Like many barons of his day, Cromwell wanted his home comforts as well as security, and inside the tower are six floors of fine chambers, each with small rooms in the corner towers. Visitors may well have the curious feeling that the rooms are getting larger as they head upwards, and this is actually the case – it was not necessary to have such thick walls in the upper floors, which were less likely to be attacked than the lower ones.

Open from April to October, daily except Monday and Tuesday. Tel: 01526 342543.

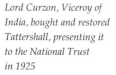
Lord Curzon, Viceroy of India, bought and restored Tattershall, presenting it to the National Trust in 1925

❖
WARWICK CASTLE
Warwickshire

WARWICK, 3 MILES (5 KM) FROM LEAMINGTON SPA

❖

The view of Warwick Castle across th e willow fringed River Avon was said by Sir Walter Scott to be unsurpassed in England

O ne of the most unpopular figures in 14th-century England was the grasping Piers Gaveston. Gaveston was the son of a Gascon knight, and attracted the attentions of Edward II long before he became king. Edward lavished titles and riches on his favourite, thereby antagonising his barons into open hostility, both against Gaveston and the King himself. Several attempts were made to banish Gaveston, but none had any lasting success. Then, in 1312, desperate measures were taken when Guy, the Earl of Warwick, and other barons seized Gaveston and took him to Warwick Castle. There, perhaps in the Great Hall, Gaveston was given a perfunctory trial and sentenced to death. He was executed on Blacklow Hill, just outside Warwick.

The powerful walls of Warwick Castle tower over the River Avon and the surrounding countryside. Because the castle has been constantly occupied since the Normans first erected a mound here, many fine buildings have been added over the centuries. Among the most magnificent are the imposing Jacobean wing and the 14th-century Guy's Tower. Inside the castle are many splendid rooms, including the State Rooms with their lavish furnishings, as well as a tasteful tableau of wax figures to recreate an actual late 19th century house party. There is an outstanding collection of arms and armour, as well as a new 'sights and sounds' exhibition, 'Warwick the Kingmaker'.

Open all year, daily except Christmas. Tel: 01926 408000.

ACTON BURNELL CASTLE
Shropshire

7 MILES (11 KM) SOUTH-EAST OF SHREWSBURY

The elegant fortified manor house of Acton Burnell is reached by a short walk from the car park along a wooded path. It is a charming ruin, standing among the trees, a quiet, peaceful place disturbed by little more than the singing of birds. Roofless, with only the walls still standing, it has large windows on the ground floor – unusual for a fortified house because the windows would have been difficult to defend if the house had ever come under attack. In times of peace, however, they had the advantage of allowing plenty of light into what would otherwise have been a rather gloomy set of ground floor rooms.

Acton Burnell was originally built as a comfortable manor house by Robert Burnell, after whom the house was named. Burnell was an important man in the 13th century, serving both as Edward I's Chancellor of England and as Bishop of Bath and Wells. Because medieval kings were usually worried about how much power their barons were amassing, no one was allowed to build a castle without the king's permission. In some cases, the king might give one of his subjects a 'licence to crenellate', which meant that an existing house might be given some defensive features, such as a new tower or battlements. In the 1280s, Robert Burnell was granted such a licence, and changed Acton Burnell from a simple dwelling place to a fortified house with battlemented parapets.

Open access at any reasonable time. Tel: 0171 973 3000.

The ruins of a fine fortified manor, Acton Burnell was abandoned in 1420

BEAUMARIS CASTLE
Gwynedd

5 MILES (8 KM) NORTH-EAST OF THE MENAI BRIDGE

The construction of Beaumaris involved a huge workforce including 400 masons and 2,000 labourers

Sitting majestically on the shores of the Menai Straits, looking from the island of Anglesey across to mainland Wales, this powerful castle took more than 35 years to build, and even so was never completely finished. It was the last of the great castles built by Edward I following his conquest of Wales, and was designed by Edward's most famous castle-builder, Master James of St George.

The building of Beaumaris Castle was started in 1295, and with its wide moat, high walls and strong towers, it was thought to be impregnable. However, this was never put to the test, and no siege machines or artillery have ever fired at this mighty fortress.

Less than 20 years after building work stopped on the still-unfinished castle, there were reports that it was already falling into decay.

Master James had not intended Beaumaris to be merely a powerful fortress, but had designed it with comfort in mind, and the inner buildings had luxurious chambers, with an extensive array of kitchens, stables and a chapel. The castle itself is in two rings, one inside the other. The inner ring has two massive twin-towered gatehouses, while the outer ring is a wall 27 feet (8.2m) high, bristling with defensive towers and its own protected dock.

Open all year daily, except Christmas and New Year. Tel: 01248 810361.

CAERPHILLY CASTLE
Mid Glamorgan

CAERPHILLY, 8 MILES (13 KM) NORTH OF CARDIFF

Below and right, Caerphilly Castle occupies a 30 acre site, making it the second largest British castle after Dover

When the huge water systems that make up some of the defences of Caerphilly Castle are taken into account, this is one of the biggest, and certainly one of the most spectacular military complexes in Britain. The sheer size of the defences at Caerphilly can only truly be appreciated from a distance, taking in the vast outer walls, the lakes and the inner concentric castle itself.

After 1066, the Normans established themselves in southern Wales, although they left the unfarmable north to the Welsh. In the mid 13th century, the last of the Welsh-born princes, Llywelyn the Last, decided that he should unite Wales under his own rule. He began to threaten the lands held by the Normans, causing Henry III to build castles to protect them. One such castle was Caerphilly, on which work started in 1268, funded by the wealthy baron Gilbert de Clare, Earl of Gloucester and Hertford. Two years later, Llywelyn attacked. How much damage was actually done to the fledgling castle is not known, but de Clare ordered that building should be completed as soon as possible. When

Llywelyn attacked again in 1271 he was repelled, and although he was said to have claimed he could have taken it in three days, Caerphilly's defences were probably sufficiently developed to render this an idle boast.

The castle itself comprises a rectangular enclosure with outer and inner walls. The inner walls contain the two great gatehouses and the remains of the hall. Here, in the heart of the castle, the living quarters were situated, along with domestic buildings such as kitchens, storerooms, a chapel, butteries and pantries. The outer walls, well fortified with towers and their own gatehouses, gave additional protection to the inner ward and were surrounded by a moat. Beyond the moat, to the east, lay a further complex of defences in the form of great walls studded with towers. The artificial lake lent protection to the north and south sides, while the west was defended by a walled island.

After the death of de Clare's son, Caerphilly passed to Hugh Despenser, the favourite of Edward II. Edward himself took refuge here from his estranged wife and her lover, although he was forced to flee when she besieged the castle, leaving behind half his treasure and most of his clothes. Cromwell ordered Caerphilly to be slighted during the Civil War.

Open all year daily, except Christmas and New Year. Tel: 01222 883143.

After the Civil War, local people came to steal Caerphilly's stones to build houses, and subsidence caused one of its towers to lean dramatically to one side.

Above and right, viewed from any angle, by day or night, Caernarfon is a most impressive sight

CAERNARFON CASTLE
Gwynedd

CAERNARFON, 7 MILES (11 KM) SOUTH-EAST OF BANGOR

*I*n 1282, Llywelyn the Last, the last native Prince of Wales, was killed in an ambush, and Welsh resistance to English occupation began to crumble. The victorious Edward I offered the Welsh a prince who was born in Wales, could speak no word of English, and whose life and reputation no one would be able to stain. He had in mind his infant son, later Edward II, who became the first English Prince of Wales. Edward was invested in Wales in 1301, and the tradition has continued ever since. In 1969, Prince Charles was invested as the current Prince of Wales in Caernarfon's courtyard, watched by a world-wide television audience of millions.

The great creamy-grey walls of Edward I's castle dominate the little market town of Caernarfon. Building started in 1283, but a decade later the unfinished fortress came under attack during a Welsh rebellion, and considerable damage was done. Believing he could not trust the native Welsh, Edward press-ganged English craftsmen and labourers to rebuild the castle, creating what still remains the grandest and most impressive of all Welsh castles. Edward intended his castle to be not only a fortress, but also the seat of his government in Wales and his own official residence there. The massive building was also a clear statement of English victory over a defeated nation.

Caernarfon Castle is shaped like an hour-glass. Great walls with stones in banded colours (inspired by the walls

While Caernarfon was the most ambitious of Edward's great castles in Wales, it was just one of 17 that Edward built, remodelled or ordered his barons to construct, between 1276 and 1296.

of Constantinople, which Edward admired while on a crusade) run between the great towers, topped by battlemented wall-walks. The defences of the castle were formidable. In order to gain access to the courtyard, visitors were obliged to cross two drawbridges, pass through five heavy doors and walk under six portcullises. The entire way was protected by arrow slits and murder-holes, through which an unpleasant array of deadly missiles could be hurled onto unwelcome guests.

Each of the towers is different. The Eagle Tower, named for the carved eagles that once adorned the turrets, had a water gate, so that supplies could be brought by sea in the event of the castle being besieged by land. The Queen's Tower contained spacious living apartments, and today houses the Royal Welch Fusiliers Museum. The Queen's Gate was also intended to provide some lavish accommodation, but it was never completed.

Open all year daily, except Christmas and New Year. Tel: 01286 677617.

CARDIFF CASTLE
South Glamorgan

CARDIFF, 21 MILES (34 KM) SOUTH-EAST OF MERTHYR TYDFIL

*T*he site of Cardiff Castle was known to the Romans, who built a fortress here. When the Normans arrived in the 11th century, they built a motte about 40 feet (12m) high, and topped it with a wooden building. Later, a twelve-sided keep was erected, and a gatehouse and stairs were added in the 15th century. Robert, the eldest son of William the Conqueror, was held prisoner here for many years by his youngest brother, Henry I, and died in Cardiff Castle in 1134.

A short distance away from the keep on the hill is a magnificent Victorian reconstruction. These buildings owe their existence to the rich 3rd Marquess of Bute. Bute had long been fascinated by history and employed William Burges, an architect who shared his love of the past, to construct a great palace in the style of a medieval castle. Burges designed rooms with intricately painted ceilings, elaborately marbled bathrooms, spiral staircases and an impressive clock tower. The Banqueting Hall is the largest room in the castle, and has a fine wooden roof, liberally decorated with brightly coloured shields. The high walls have murals showing scenes from the Civil War, as well as a small painting of the Conqueror's son, Robert, gazing wistfully from behind his barred prison window.

Open all year, daily except Christmas and New Year. Tel: 01222 822083.

Cardiff Castle is a romantic Victorian re-creation of the Middle Ages

CAREW CASTLE
Dyfed

CAREW, 5 MILES (8 KM) EAST OF PEMBROKE

The stately ruins of Carew Castle, scene in 1507 of the last medieval tournament to be held in Wales

Although today Carew appears to be more of a palace than a castle, it still possesses some of its original defensive features. Of these, perhaps the most impressive are the two great cylindrical towers with their jutting bases. Parts of the medieval castle were altered in the 15th and 16th centuries, when its many different owners built new wings and exchanged the small, narrow windows for larger, stately ones.

One of Carew's first owners is said to have been Gerald of Windsor, who was married to a Welsh princess named Nest. Before her marriage, Nest had been a hostage of Henry I, and legend has it that she bore his illegitimate son. Nest's grandson was Gerald of Wales, whose detailed description of life in the 12th century is an important source of information for medieval historians.

Another legend attached to Carew is that of Sir Roland Rhys, who lived in the castle during the reign of James I. When his son eloped with the daughter of a Flemish merchant, Rhys attacked the merchant with his pet ape. Later, the ape attacked Rhys himself, and during the struggle which followed, the castle caught fire. However, the most serious damage to be inflicted on Carew's elegant buildings occurred during the Civil War.

Open Easter to October, daily. Tel: 01646 651657/651782.

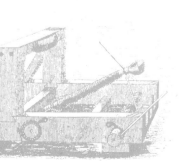

CARREG CENNEN CASTLE
Dyfed

NEAR LLANDEILO, 16 MILES (26 KM) EAST OF CARMARTHEN

Carreg Cennen's walls command wonderful views across to the Black Mountains

Perched on a limestone crag, Carreg Cennen overlooks miles of rolling Welsh countryside. Steep cliffs and slopes protect the castle on three sides, while the one vulnerable approach is well defended with walls, watchtowers, pits and gates.

Roman coins have been found at Carreg Cennen, suggesting that the site was a fortress long before the present buildings were erected. The original Welsh castle was demolished in the 13th century to make way for the complex, heavily fortified buildings that remain today. It suffered extensive damage, first at the hands of Owain Glyndwr in the 14th century and then by the Yorkists during the Wars of the Roses in the 15th century.

Under the castle, burrowed into the rock itself, is a huge natural cavern, reached from the castle by a narrow, vaulted passageway along the edge of the cliff. Although water drips almost constantly into the cave at one end, it would have been insufficient to supply a whole garrison, and the passage was probably built to ensure that invaders could not use the cave as a point from which to attack the castle. It would appear that at one time the passage was used as a dovecote, presumably to supply the castle kitchens.

Open all year daily, except Christmas and New Year. Tel: 01558 822291.

❊
CASTELL-Y-BERE
Gwynedd

9 MILES (14.5 KM) SOUTH OF DOLGELLAU
❊

Abandoned in this remote area, Castell-y-Bere has been left to deteriorate since the 13th century

The site of this once-powerful Welsh-built castle is dwarfed by the mountains that tower over it. Cader Idris is one of the great peaks looming steeply over the site of Castell-y-Bere. The castle is reached by a path that leads around the rocky spur on which it is perched, and approaching from this angle gives an accurate impression of the natural strength of the site. Castell-y-Bere once controlled one of the primary routes through central Wales, but today the major road runs further south and the castle is abandoned and lonely.

Little remains, and most of the buildings are represented by foundations alone. It was originally built by Llywelyn the Great in the 1220s, probably more to secure his position as Prince of Wales against his warring compatriots than to stand against the invading Normans. The castle was roughly triangular, following the shape of the rock, with towers at each angle. The entrance was defended by an impressive array of ditches, as well as a drawbridge and a portcullis.

During Edward I's wars against the Welsh princes, Castell-y-Bere was besieged and damaged. Although Edward paid more than £260 to have the castle repaired, it was not occupied for long, and was abandoned by about 1295.

Open access at any reasonable time. Tel: 01222 465511.

Marten's Tower at Chepstow is named after Henry Marten, one of the Cromwellians who signed Charles I's death warrant. Marten was held prisoner here after the monarchy had been restored.

CHEPSTOW CASTLE
Gwent

15 MILES (24 KM) EAST OF NEWPORT

Below and right, Chepstow Castle stands in a strategic position above the River Wye

Chepstow was one of the first stone castles ever to be built in Britain. It was started in 1068, a mere two years after the invasion of England by William the Conqueror. William knew that in order to continue to hold what he had acquired at the Battle of Hastings, it was necessary to dominate the newly conquered people with a show of Norman power. This was achieved by castle building – at first simple mounds topped with wooden structures, and later, more permanent stone towers.

Chepstow was of great strategic importance, and William entrusted one of his best generals, William FitzOsbern, to build the castle and control the Marches. FitzOsbern chose a site that was naturally protected on one side by cliffs plummeting down into the brown waters of the Wye, and on another by a valley. He protected the remaining sides with stone walls. The very first building was a simple two-storeyed rectangular keep with some fine arched windows.

Around 1190, Chepstow passed to the Marshall family, who set about improving defences by adding strong curtain walls with towers set into them. They extended the castle too, and these alterations divided the castle into four separate sections, each leading into the other from east to west. The Marshalls were also responsible for the imposing gate-house that looms over present-day visitors as they enter the castle. The gatehouse has a prison in one of its round towers, a dismal chamber with only an airshaft to break the monotony of the dank walls.

After 1270 a second hall, a D-shaped tower and another gatehouse were

built on by one of Edward I's most powerful barons, Roger Bigod. Bigod's buildings contain comfortable living quarters, well-equipped with kitchens, larders, and storerooms. A double-seated latrine was also provided for visitors to the hall, and its waste was discharged down the steep cliffs above the river.

Although Chepstow was never besieged in medieval times, it played an important role in the Civil War, coming under siege twice while it was being held for King Charles I. The garrison surrendered the first time, but fell after a fierce battle on the second occasion. After the Civil War, its importance gradually declined, and it began to fall into the romantic ruin it is today.

Open all year daily, except Christmas and New Year. Tel: 01291 624065.

CASTELL COCH
South Glamorgan

TONGWYNLAIS, 6 MILES (9.5 KM) NORTH-WEST OF CARDIFF

Secure on its wooded hillside, Castell Coch is more like a French château than a traditional British castle

Rising out of wooded parklands, and clearly visible from the main road from Cardiff to Pontypridd, stands Castell Coch, a vast, elegant building with conical towers and a working drawbridge. Castell Coch, meaning 'red castle' in Welsh (it is built of red sandstone), is just like a castle from some fairy-tale. It was built during the 19th century, at a time when Victorians were expressing a great interest in the past, especially in the seemingly idyllic, industry-free Middle Ages.

Castell Coch was designed by the architect William Burges for the 3rd Marquess of Bute, and it was not the first time these two men had worked together. They were also responsible for work on Cardiff Castle, with Bute providing the fortune and Burges the plans. Castell Coch was never intended to be a permanent residence, but was, in Burges' words, 'for occasional occupation in the summer'. It even has a dungeon, but the only prisoners have been actors, since Castell Coch has proved to be a popular ready-made film set.

If the exterior of the castle is impressive, the interior is a breath-taking jumble of rich colours and minute detail. There are fabulously decorated ceilings in many rooms, while others boast intricately painted wall-panels. The total effect is the kind of exuberant gaudiness that is indisputably Victorian.

Open all year daily, except Christmas and New Year. Tel: 01222 810101.

CONWY CASTLE
Gwynedd

CONWY, 4 MILES (6.5 KM) SOUTH OF LLANDUDNO

*E*ight massive round towers and two barbicans linked by thick walls form the castle at Conwy, which, although perhaps overshadowed by Caernarfon, is one of the most spectacular in Wales.

Building at Conwy began in 1283 and was completed around 1287. During this very short time, the town's defences were also built, taking in some ¾ mile (1.2km) of walls with 22 towers and three gateways. Conwy was Edward I's most expensive Welsh castle and was designed by his talented castle architect Master James of St George. Although Conwy's eight circular towers are its most dominant feature, there are the remains of other buildings in the two wards. One is the huge Great Hall, which would have been the heart of the medieval castle, where meals were eaten and audiences held, and where some people would have slept.

Shortly after Conwy was built, there was a Welsh rebellion led by Prince Madog, and a number of Edward I's castles were badly damaged. Edward marched to Wales to supress the rebellion, setting up his headquarters at Conwy. However, as soon as he was inside the castle, the river flooded, trapping Edward and his men inside. They were stranded for several days, and supplies of food and fresh water became dangerously low before the waters receded and they were able to escape.

Open all year daily, except Christmas and New Year. Tel: 01492 592358.

Conwy Castle, seen from across the river, with the foothills of Snowdonia providing a magnificent backdrop

CRICCIETH CASTLE
Gwynedd

CRICCIETH, 5 MILES (8 KM) WEST OF PORTHMADOG

*I*n 1404 Criccieth Castle was taken from the English by Owain Glyndwr, the last of the Welsh leaders to rebel against the English crown. Shortly afterwards, the castle was so badly damaged by fire that it was never used again. In the 1930s, an archaeological investigation found proof of the fire that brought the castle's role in history to such an abrupt end, when charred timbers were discovered dating to the 15th century.

Criccieth, like many castles, was built in several different stages. The first stage, which included the solid twin-towered gatehouse, was built by Llywelyn the Great, while his grandson, Llywelyn the Last, added more walls and a rectangular tower. Edward I took the castle after Llywelyn the Last's defeat, and ordered the building of more walls and a tower strong enough to mount a siege engine on the roof.

Today, Criccieth is in ruins, although its commanding position on a promontory overlooking the picturesque Tremadog Bay, gives an idea of the status this castle must once have enjoyed. Llywelyn the Great's massive gatehouse still presents a forbidding face to the world, and the thickness of its crumbling walls still imbue it with an aura of strength and permanence.

Open all year daily, except Christmas and New Year. Tel: 01766 522227.

Criccieth sits neatly above the little town

❊

DENBIGH CASTLE
Clwyd

DENBIGH, 9 MILES (14.5 KM) NORTH-WEST OF RUTHIN

❊

Denbigh Castle was once occupied by Sir Henry Percy – the Hotspur of Shakespeare's Henry IV plays

Standing among the crumbling walls of Denbigh Castle, it is not difficult to imagine the former splendour and power of this now ruined castle. It sits on top of a hill overlooking the town, commanding fine views of the surrounding countryside, and even in decay, still exudes a feeling of Norman dominance.

Denbigh's most impressive feature is its great gatehouse, although the centuries have not treated it kindly. It was almost triangular, and was made up of three interlinked octagonal towers. The front part has an elegant arched door, while the stonework around it is of an unusual chequered pattern made up of different coloured stones. Above the door there is a niche that still holds a statue of Edward I, now very weathered.

Because Edward I's funds for castle building were not unlimited, he persuaded as many of his barons as he could to build castles for him. Denbigh was such a castle, and was built between 1282 and 1311 by Henry de Lacey, Earl of Lincoln. An unusual feature is the steep sloping barbican that protected the back of the castle.

Denbigh's most famous son, Henry Morton Stanley (1841–1904), the journalist-turned-explorer, spent his early years living in a cottage on the castle grounds.

Open all year daily, except Christmas and New Year. Tel: 01745 813979.

*Dolbadarn Castle overlooks
the waters of Llyn Peris*

DOLBADARN CASTLE
Gwynedd

7½ MILES (12 KM) EAST OF CAERNARFON

Huge steep-sided mountains loom on both sides of the Llanberis Pass as the road winds down towards Caernarfon and the coast. Here can be found Dolbadarn Castle, still standing sentinel to the route it once guarded. Although Dolbadarn was never large, it was of great importance to the Welsh princes. When Llywelyn the Last retreated to his mountain stronghold to escape from Edward I, the Llanberis Pass was the main route to the farmlands of Anglesey, whence most of Llywelyn's supplies came.

The castle's most striking feature is the single round tower that still survives to a height of 40 feet (12m). The entry was on the first floor, with wooden steps that could be pulled up inside the castle in the event of an attack. It was probably built by Llywelyn the Great in the early 13th century, and is much stronger and better built than the rest of the castle, of which little remains but the foundations. One of the most remarkable aspects of Dolbadarn is its contrasting views. On one side lie the gently undulating hills with the lake twinkling in the distance, while on the other stand the stark mountains of the Snowdonia National Park, some ripped open by slate quarriers.

Open all year, daily. Tel: 01286 870377.

DOLWYDDELAN CASTLE
Gwynedd

DOLWYDDELAN, 6 MILES (10 KM) SOUTH-WEST OF BETWS-Y-COED

This sturdy three-storeyed tower appears almost insignificant among the sweeping hills of the Welsh countryside, especially next to the rugged green-brown slopes of Moal-Siabod that lie to one side. The precise origins of the castle are obscured by time, but it was built by the Princes of Wales to guard the ancient pathway that ran from Merionnydd to the Vale of Conwy. It may have been built by Iorwerth Trwyndwn ('the flat-nosed'), and it is said that one of Wales' most famous princes, Llywelyn the Great, was born here around 1173. Edward I's forces attacked it in 1283 during his Welsh campaign, and seeing its great strategic value, the King had it refortified and manned by English soldiers: thus the Welsh-built castle became a stronghold for the English.

The castle itself was originally a rectangular tower of two storeys; it was later given an extra floor and a battlemented roof line. Later still, thick walls were added to form an enclosure with another rectangular tower, all protected by ditches cut into the rock. Although it was built by the Welsh, the architect of Dolwyddelan borrowed heavily from the Norman style of castle-building, and there was a door on the first floor, protected by a drawbridge.

Open open all year daily, except at Christmas and New Year. Tel: 016906 366.

Dolwyddelan Castle is reputedly the birthplace of Llewelyn the Great

*Above and right, a red
sandstone ruin, Goodrich
Castle has wonderful views in
all directions*

GOODRICH CASTLE
Hereford & Worcester

GOODRICH, 6 MILES (10 KM) NORTH-EAST OF MONMOUTH

For first-time visitors to Goodrich Castle, a great surprise lies in store. Goodrich is approached from the car park through a line of trees, and it is not until you are quite close that the full splendour of this magnificent fortress can be appreciated.

Goodrich does not possess the elegance or the picturesque quality of some castles – it was built for strength and defence. However, time has given these ruins a beauty their builders never intended and Goodrich today is one of the castles which are most evocative of Norman dominance.

In the middle of the 12th century the first stone building at Goodrich was raised – a sturdy, pale-red keep. It stands 60 feet (18m) high today, although it was originally taller and would probably have had battlements. In the late 13th century the de Valence family, who owned the castle, decided to turn the simple keep

that the castle archers could fire their deadly weapons at attackers without being exposed themselves.

The gatehouse tower also housed a chapel, and the rounded end of this building can still be seen. Inside the thick walls are a range of domestic buildings that would have made castle life relatively comfortable. There was a large hall, a solar and kitchen buildings. Despite these features, Goodrich Castle was intended first and foremost as a defensive building, and, in its prime, Goodrich must have been a formidable fortress indeed.

Open April to September daily, closed on winter Mondays and Tuesdays, and at Christmas and New Year. Tel: 01600 890538.

Murder holes, or gaps through which defenders could drop a variety of objects, such as stones and even kitchen waste, were a common feature of medieval castles. Although a popular image is of boiling oil being dropped onto attackers, both oil and the fuel to heat it were valuable commodities and it is very unlikely that these would have been wasted in this way.

into a formidable fortress. Round the keep, they built four massive walls. At three of the corners were cylindrical towers with great square bases that seem to grow out of the rock on which they are anchored. Undermining these towers would have been extremely difficult, especially as the whole castle was surrounded by a deep moat.

The fourth corner had a huge gatehouse tower that led out into the barbican. This barbican was a semicircular enclosure and forced any would-be attackers to make a rightangled turn to gain access to the castle proper. This change in direction was intended to slow the attackers down, thus exposing them to the arrows and missiles of the defenders. Gates, drawbridges and portcullises were used for the same purpose, well provided with nearby arrow slits, so

FLINT CASTLE
Clwyd

FLINT, 10 MILES (16 KM) NORTH-WEST OF CHESTER

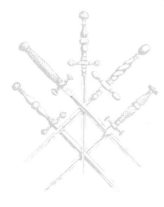

*Once an important fortress,
Flint Castle stands deserted
by past and present*

In August 1399 King Richard II, fleeing from the forces of his cousin Henry of Bolingbrooke, arrived at Flint Castle. Within days, Bolingbrooke had captured Richard and had him taken to London, where he abdicated in Bolingbrooke's favour. Bolingbrooke became King Henry IV, while Richard was eventually taken to Pontefract castle in Yorkshire, where he was probably murdered.

Flint was the first of the castles built by Edward I during his Welsh campaigns. Building started in 1277 with an enormous workforce of 2300 labourers, who were paid handsomely, since building a castle in a hostile land was not popular work. The castle consisted of a rectangular enclosure with four round towers at the corners. This was further protected by additional walls, a moat and some deep ditches. One of the round corner towers was larger than the others, and was protected by its own moat. It also had its own kitchens, living quarters and chapel, and was probably the residence of the constable and his family.

Nowadays, this once vitally important castle is hidden behind the modern town, bypassed by tourists heading west and standing lonely and forgotten on the marshy shores of the River Dee.

Open access at any reasonable time. Cadw, tel: 01222 500261.

A section of the old walls of Grosmont

GROSMONT CASTLE
Gwent

GROSMONT, 12 MILES (19 KM) NORTH-WEST OF MONMOUTH

Three castles – Grosmont, Skenfrith, and White – were built by the Normans to protect this important sector of the Marches. At first, the castles were only wooden structures strengthened by earthworks. But continued Welsh rebellion against Norman rule meant that more permanent fortresses were needed, and one of King John's barons, Hubert de Burgh, Earl of Kent, set out to provide them. However, the favour of medieval kings was an uncertain thing to hold, and Hubert lost his Three Castles twice during his chequered career.

Thus the Three Castles had at least two main building phases. Hubert started the first stone building at Grosmont in 1201, mainly comprising the rectangular hall. When Hubert held the Three Castles for the second time, between 1219 and 1232, he added a gatehouse and the round towers.

Grosmont has seen some action in its 800-year history. It was attacked by the Welsh in 1233, and Owain Glyndwr laid seige to it in 1405. Grosmont is also associated with Jack O'Kent, a local folk hero. Legend has it that the devil had promised to take O'Kent, whether he was buried in the church or outside it. O'Kent's grave is under the wall of the village church, so that he was neither inside nor out.

Open access all year. Tel: 01981 240301.

Edward I's Welsh Castles

*E*dward Longshanks, the tall, golden-haired warrior who ruled England from 1272 to 1307, was perhaps one of the most powerful English kings in history. Throughout the reign of his father, Henry III, the Scots had engaged in a series of border wars with the English, and the Welsh had made quite serious bids for independence. Edward determined to put an end to this and crushed them both ruthlessly, earning himself the title 'Hammer of the Scots' and leaving behind a string of powerful fortresses in Wales.

Edward's chief opponent in Wales was Llywelyn the Last, so called because with his death, the line of Welsh-born princes came to an end. Llywelyn's wars with Edward came in two phases, each resulting in a frenzy of castle building on Edward's part. The first confrontations occurred in 1276 and 1277. Llywelyn had married the daughter of Edward's enemy Simon de Montfort and was openly refusing to pay homage to Edward. The King acted quickly and effectively, swooping down on Wales and driving Llywelyn into his Gwynedd stronghold. Llywelyn had no option but to yield, and all his lands outside Gwynedd were forfeit to Edward.

In order to consolidate what he had won, Edward began to build castles. He employed one of the greatest military architects ever to have lived: Master James of St George, a mason from the French-Swiss border who had already gained considerable experience of castle building in France. Edward and Master James constructed castles at Flint and Rhuddlan, and fortified already existing castles at Builth and Aberystwyth. Ruthin and Hawarden were also raised.

The sight of these English-built fortresses on Welsh land naturally gave rise to discontent. In 1282, Llywelyn's unpredictable brother, Daffydd, revolted and Llywelyn rallied to his people's call for him to lead them against English repression. Edward put down the rebellion even more ruthlessly than before. Llywelyn was killed in an ambush in December 1282, and with his death, Welsh resistance began to crumble.

Right, Edward I was to become the scourge of the Welsh

Edward's great castles are all in North Wales, since this was where Llywelyn's rebellion was based, but there are equally impressive castles in South Wales too. These include Pembroke, Caerphilly and Kidwelly, built by wealthy barons rather than by the King himself.

Left, while the castle at Denbigh was allowed to fall into ruin, Chirk, below left, survived to be completely remodelled in the nineteenth century

Edward stormed into Wales, taking Dolwyddelan, Dolbadarn, and Castell-y-Bere. This time, Edward ensured that no further rebellions could take place in North Wales, and Master James was ordered to design castles at Conwy, Harlech, and Beaumaris. Edward paid for Caernarfon, while Denbigh, Holt and Chirk were paid for by Edward's nobles. Already existing Welsh-built castles at Criccieth and Caergwle were repaired and strengthened. Edward's North Wales castles display some of the most splendid military architecture in the world. They are stark symbols of Edward's dominance over a defeated nation, but at the same time are magnificent illustrations of medieval life in Wales.

The remarkable 'Way of the Sea' is a fortified stairway leading from Harlech Castle down to where the sea once lapped at the edge of the cliffs. This meant the castle could be supplied by ships if the land was blockaded.

HARLECH CASTLE
Gwynedd

HARLECH, 16 MILES (25.5 KM) SOUTH OF PORTHMADOG

The last great uprising of the Welsh against the occupying English occurred in the early 15th century under the leadership of the great hero Owain Glyndwr. In the spring of 1404, Glyndwr gathered his forces against the mighty fortress of Harlech, but the castle was too strong to be taken in a battle and so Glyndwr began a siege. For many months the castle garrison held out, despite Glyndwr's efficient blockade of all the castle's supply routes. Food began to run low, and then disease broke out, doubtless aggravated by the shortage of clean water for drinking, cooking and washing. After some of the soldiers had made an unsuccessful attempt to escape, Glyndwr stood at the castle's gate and demanded surrender.

Harlech was Glyndwr's home and headquarters for the next four years, and it is possible he even held a Welsh parliament there. It is also said that he crowned himself Prince of Wales in Harlech. Finally, in 1409, Henry IV sent a powerful force to recapture the castle and stamp out the rebellion. After a short siege, the castle fell. Glyndwr's wife and children were taken prisoner, and although Glyndwr himself escaped, the fall of Harlech marked the beginning of the end for him. Within four years he had disappeared.

The great castle that allowed its garrison to withstand intense and prolonged sieges was one of Edward I's 'iron ring' of castles built during his second castle building campaign. Unlike Beaumaris, on which building continued for 35 years, Harlech was completed within seven years (1283–1290). Master James of St George personally supervised the building, and it does not take much imagination to envisage what a remarkable feat of engineering was required to erect such a vast fortress in such a short space of time.

Harlech is concentric, with outer walls giving further protection to the inner walls, which contained the main living quarters. The inner walls also contain the great gatehouse, with its comfortable residential apartments. The gatehouse is perhaps Harlech's finest feature, a vast structure that presents a forbidding display of thick grey walls and impregnability. Harlech's mighty walls were not its only defence. Two sides were protected by deep dry moats hacked out of the rock on which the castle stands, while cliffs plunging down to the sea made assault on the back of the castle virtually impossible.

Open all year daily, except Christmas and New Year. Tel: 01766 780552.

Below and left, rising 200ft on a rocky promontory, the striking castle at Harlech remains largely intact

KIDWELLY CASTLE
Dyfed

KIDWELLY, 9 MILES (14.5 KM) WEST OF LLANELLI

The early history of this well-preserved castle was tempestuous. Roger, the Bishop of Salisbury, put up earthworks on the site, some of which can still be seen in the semi-circular ditch that curves around the present castle. In 1231, Llywelyn the Great attacked the Norman castle, causing considerable damage. Its owner, Patrick de Chaworth, rebuilt the castle and it withstood another attack in the 1250s. Most of the building that remains today, however, dates from the 1270s.

The main castle forms a rectangle, with great circular towers at each corner. A semi-circular wall sweeps around one side and the site is protected by defensive earthworks. Unusually, the great gatehouse is not a part of the inner walls, as in other castles, but rather forms part of the outer walls. The most likely reason for this is that there was not enough firm ground inside the castle to support such a large building.

The many small rooms and chambers in the walls and towers of Kidwelly, and the narrow interconnecting passages and stairs, give a particularly vivid sense of what life must have been like in a medieval castle.

Open all year daily, except Christmas and New Year. Tel: 01554 890104.

The great gatehouse at Kidwelly was strong opposition for any attacker

LAUGHARNE CASTLE
Dyfed

LAUGHARNE, 14 MILES (22 KM) SOUTH-WEST OF CARMARTHEN

Laugharne Castle, once a place for battles and sieges, is now just a romantic shell

The Laugharne Castle that can be seen today bears very little resemblance to the building that was erected in the 12th century. This original castle was seized from the English by Welsh princes three times before the end of the 13th century: by Rhys ap Gruffydd, Llywelyn the Great, and Llywelyn the Last. Parts of the ivy-clad building that can be visited today date from the early 14th century, and the gatehouse is thought to be 15th century. The grand entrance arch in the gateway was added later still, probably during the 16th century.

In Tudor times, Laugharne was leased to Sir John Perrott, said to be the illegitimate son of Henry VIII, who did not find the medieval castle to his courtly taste and set about converting it into a fine Tudor mansion. The foundations of his hall can be seen in the courtyard near the well.

Laugharne Castle came under siege during the Civil War, and some of the cannonballs fired at it by the Round-heads have been found deeply embedded in its sturdy stone battlements. The small town of Laugharne is perhaps best known for its associations with the poet Dylan Thomas.

Under restoration; for the latest information contact Cadw, tel: 01222 465511.

LLANSTEFFAN CASTLE
Dyfed

LLANSTEFFAN, 8 MILES (13 KM) SOUTH-WEST OF CARMARTHEN

Running like a finger across the gently undulating farmland of the Dyfed coast is a ridge that ends in a rocky bluff. The advantages of this site for defence were recognised long before the Normans arrived, and charcoal from an iron age hill fort has been dated to the 6th century BC.

When the Normans established themselves in Wales, they were quick to make use of this ready-made site, protected on three sides by natural slopes, and a ditch was dug to strengthen the fourth side. The castle has two baileys, or enclosed areas. The smaller area is the older of the two, and the small square tower, which can still be seen, was defended by battlemented walls.

When the Welsh took Llansteffan in 1257 (with embarrassing ease), the English de Camville family decided to make improvements to the castle's defences. They built thick walls around the lower bailey, as well as several towers and a fine gatehouse. In Tudor times the gatehouse was converted from a functional military building into a comfortable residence. Before Llansteffan came into the hands of Cadw to be carefully restored as an historic monument, it was used as farm buildings for some 400 years.

Open access all year. Tel: 0126783 756.

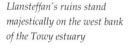

Llansteffan's ruins stand majestically on the west bank of the Towy estuary

A view of the castle and its surroundings from the top of the keep

LUDLOW CASTLE
Shropshire

LUDLOW, 12 MILES (19.5 KM) NORTH OF LEOMINSTER

Throughout 1138, England was wracked by a civil war fought between supporters of King Stephen and his cousin Empress Matilda, both of whom thought they were rightful heirs to the English throne. Stephen laid siege to the castle at Ludlow, which was then held by one of Matilda's supporters. While he was walking outside the castle walls with Prince Henry of Scotland, a metal hook on a rope was lowered from the castle, catching on the Prince's cloak. As the Prince began to rise up the walls, quick-thinking Stephen cut the rope and managed to free him. He did not, however, take the castle, and was forced to abandon his siege and fight elsewhere.

The extensive ruins of Ludlow Castle contain much that is interesting or unusual. There is a circular chapel modelled on the Church of the Holy Sepulchre in Jerusalem, one of only six round churches in England. There are curtain walls with flanking towers that are among the earliest such defensive features in England, and a gatehouse that was later blocked up to make a square tower and then, later still, reduced in size. Many of the existing domestic buildings, such as the kitchens, halls, and service rooms, were built in the 14th century, but were given Tudor facelifts.

Open from February to November, daily. Tel: 01584 873947.

MANORBIER CASTLE
Dyfed

MANORBIER, 5½ MILES (9 KM) SOUTH-WEST OF TENBY

The lovely old castle of Manorbier was the birthplace of Giraldus Cambrensis

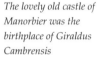

The strong limestone walls of Manorbier Castle have weathered the centuries well and still stand largely intact after 800 years. The first stone buildings were a three-storeyed square tower and a long hall. In the 13th century the curtain walls were raised, with flanking towers and a fine gatehouse. Two large barns were built in the castle in the 17th century. Manorbier's considerable defences, including the sturdy walls, battlements, portcullises and ditches, were never put to the test by a serious siege, and the Norman de Barri family lived their lives happily unassailed by attacks from the local Welsh people.

Manorbier Castle is perhaps most famous as the birthplace of Giraldus Cambrensis, or Gerald of Wales as he is also known. Gerald was a scholar who travelled extensively before he became an archdeacon, and his sensitive and incisive observations provide a valuable record of life in medieval Wales and Ireland. Beside his analyses of Welsh politics and history, he described the people and their way of life – how they slept on communal beds of rushes wearing all their clothes, and how their feuding and vengeful natures were balanced by their love of music and poetry.

Open from Easter to September, daily. Tel: 01834 871317/871394.

PEMBROKE CASTLE
Dyfed

PEMBROKE, 10 MILES (16 KM) SOUTH EAST OF MILFORD HAVEN

It was at Pembroke Castle in the 15th century that Henry Tudor was born in the tower named after him

Pembroke Castle's most outstanding feature is its great tower – a vast circular keep that stands almost 80 feet (24m) high, with walls that are 16½ feet (5m) at the thickest part, all capped by an unusual stone dome. Although the keep once had four floors, these have long since disappeared, and today you can stand in the basement and gaze all the way up to the stone dome itself. The great tower was built between 1200 and 1210, probably by William Marshall, one of Richard I's most powerful barons.

There are two other unusual features to note about this castle. The first is the medieval graffiti scored into the plaster walls of the Monkton Tower, and the second is the 'Wogan', a great natural cavern under the castle that can be reached by a spiral stair.

The rest of the castle – great battlemented walls liberally studded with defensive towers and a mighty gatehouse – was besieged by Cromwell during the Civil War. Once the defending garrison had surrendered, Cromwell blew up the barbican and some of the towers to ensure that Pembroke Castle could not become a refuge for Royalist forces again. Much of the castle was restored during the last century.

Open all year daily, except Christmas and New Year. Tel: 01646 681510.

William Marshall (*c*1146–1219) once defeated Richard the Lionheart in a fight and could have killed him. Years later, Richard remembered Marshall's act of mercy and made him the Earl of Pembroke.

PENHOW CASTLE
Gwent

PENHOW, 10 MILES (16 KM) SOUTH-WEST OF CHEPSTOW

Penhow is believed to be the oldest inhabited castle in Wales

*P*enhow Castle, the home of the powerful Seymour family, was originally a simple Norman tower of three storeys. The roof was battlemented and the walls were six feet (1.8m) thick, making this attractive building more of a fortified manor house than a castle. Recent excavations have uncovered a ditch cut out of the rock, which served as a small dry moat providing the castle with additional protection. In the 15th century a hall was added at right angles to the early tower, above which is the Great Chamber, a room that was probably used by the lord of the manor and his family as sleeping quarters. The hall itself is a light and airy room.

The current owners of Penhow Castle have gone to some trouble to ensure that as much as possible of the medieval atmosphere of these buildings has been retained, and have furnished it much as it would have been in medieval times.

The final stage in the building of this small but complex castle was a 17th-century house which adjoins the other buildings. This has ornate moulded plaster ceilings, some elegantly carved wooden panels, and door surrounds inset with intricate paintings of landscapes.

Open from Easter to September on most days, and Wednesdays in winter. Tel: 01633 400800.

RHUDDLAN CASTLE
Clwyd

RHUDDLAN, 3 MILES (5 KM) SOUTH OF RHYL

*Rhuddlan Castle towers
majestically over the
River Clwyd*

This concentric castle was built by Edward I, but now stands uncomfortably next to a modern housing development. Its once-powerful round towers are crumbling around their bases, and time has eaten away at their roofless tops. Yet Rhuddlan was a vitally important part of Edward I's campaign in Wales and was designed by his master castle-builder James of St George. Indeed, it was here that the Great Statute of Wales was issued in March 1284, proclaiming Edward's dominance over the defeated country.

Rhuddlan Castle is diamond-shaped with towers at each corner, and has two sets of outer walls. It also has its own dock tower. The building of the castle in its present location necessitated a great feat of military engineering. The site was already historically important because it was on a ford over the River Clwyd. Edward wanted his new castle to have access to the sea, so that it might be supplied by boats, but the Clywd was a shallow river that meandered lazily towards the sea. Edward cut a new channel, which was deeper and straighter than the one the river had made for itself, and 700 years later it still more or less follows this course.

Open all year daily, except Christmas and New Year. Tel: 01745 590777.

RAGLAN CASTLE
Gwent

RAGLAN, 7 MILES (11 KM) SOUTH-WEST OF MONMOUTH

*I*t is said that Charles I played bowls on the grass on Raglan's terraces, under the shadow of the great Yellow Tower of Gwent, the most imposing part of this magnificent 15th-century castle. The story goes that the local bowls champion was called to provide an able competitor, and horrifed the King's class-conscious entourage by proudly pointing out his house in the village.

A short time later, the country was at war, and Charles relied on more from Raglan and his Welsh subjects than a good game of bowls. At that time, Raglan was owned by the Earl of Worcester, who immediately gar-risoned the castle for the King. Cromwellian forces laid siege to the castle in June 1646, and the powerful walls underwent weeks of devast-ating bombardment. On 19 August Worcester was forced to surrender, and Cromwell's troops poured into the castle. Worcester was taken to London, where he died shortly after, and Raglan Castle was stripped of anything portable and left derelict. Further destruction took place after the Restoration, when the newly created Duke of Beaufort ransacked Raglan for fittings for his new home at Badminton. By the 19th century, Raglan was a romantic ivy-clad ruin.

There had been a castle at Raglan since about 1070, and there are records to suggest that the original castle survived until well into the early 1400s. This building fell into the hands of William ap Thomas, a Welsh knight who had fought at the Battle of Agincourt with Henry V. Thomas began to build a tower in an unusual hexagonal shape, a four-storeyed keep with thick, tapering walls. He surrounded the tower with more walls and a moat, and the pale gold stone from which it is built earned it its name: the Yellow Tower of Gwent. Thomas' son William, Earl of Pembroke, continued the building work, and added the Pitched Stone Court and the Great Gatehouse. He also rebuilt much of the Fountain Court, and made it into gracious living quarters for his family. William, a Yorkist, was defeated at the Battle of Edgecote, and was executed by Warwick, 'The Kingmaker'.

Standing between Raglan's two courtyards is the Great Hall, mainly Elizabethan in origin. Worcester entertained on a lavish scale here, and it is easy to imagine these grand occasions with his guests sitting at long tables, and the fine stained glass casting patterned light into the room.

Open all year daily, except Christmas and New Year. Tel: 01291 690228.

The handsome ruins of Raglan Castle can be seen from several miles away

TRETOWER CASTLE & COURT
Powys

TRETOWER, 3½ MILES (6 KM) NORTH-WEST OF CRICKHOWELL

*T*here was a Norman castle on this site as early as AD1100, consisting of a mound with a wooden structure perched on top. This was converted to a stone building in the 12th century, and thick walls were added. At this point it was discovered that the castle's water supply was seeping below the mound and undermining it, and so additional stone foundations had to be laid to prevent subsidence.

In the early 13th century, this castle was pulled down and a circular tower built in its place. It had walls that were nine feet (2.7m) thick, and the bottom splayed outwards to make it more difficult to undermine. This stalwart round tower, with its small Norman arched windows, still stands among the trees of the beautiful Usk Valley.

In the early 15th century Tretower Court was rebuilt on the site of an earlier house by its owner, Sir Robert Vaughan. The Court, with its magnificent wooden-ceilinged hall, remained the home of the Vaughan family until 1783. The buildings are still well preserved, although parts have been reconstructed. The sliding shutters in the gallery and the elegant wood-panelled partition are of particular interest.

Open all year daily, except Christmas and New Year. Tel: 01874 730279.

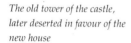
The old tower of the castle, later deserted in favour of the new house

WHITE CASTLE
Gwent

7 MILES (11 KM) NORTH-EAST OF ABERGAVENNY

White Castle was one of a formidable trio built to defend the Welsh Marches

White Castle gained its name from the white plaster that once covered it, but only traces of this can be seen today on the castle's crumbling walls. White's sister castles, Grosmont and Skenfrith, were built by Hubert de Burgh. While he owned the so-called Three Castles of Gwent between 1201 and 1204 and from 1219 to 1232, White itself had a rather different origin.

Like Skenfrith and Grosmont, White Castle began as earthworks with wooden buildings. In the 12th century, a stone curtain wall was added, and in the 13th century a gatehouse and additional towers were built. White Castle was near land claimed by Llywelyn the Last during his wars with Edward I, and the King ensured that its defences were strengthened. Even in its ruined state, the complexity and sophistication of the castle's defences can be appreciated, especially the height and strength of the great walls.

In 1941, Rudolf Hess, Hitler's second in command, flew to Scotland to try to negotiate a peace treaty with Great Britain. Treated as a prisoner of war, he was held for a while at a hospital near White Castle, and was taken sometimes to feed the swans in the castle moat.

Open all year daily, except Christmas and New Year. Tel: 0160085 380.

Alnwick Castle has fierce, life-like stone figures all along its battlements, perhaps to encourage invaders to believe that there were more troops in the castle than was actually the case.

ALNWICK CASTLE
Northumberland

ALNWICK, 20 MILES (32 KM) NORTH OF MORPETH

The clustered towers of this magnificent residential fortress have seen a good deal of action since the castle was founded in the 11th century. Its position near the border with Scotland made it vulnerable to attack from the Scots, and it played an important role in the Wars of the Roses during the 15th century. In 1172 and 1174 William the Lion, King of Scotland, laid siege to Alnwick, but on the second occasion he was surprised by reinforcements from the south and was himself taken prisoner. Since the early 14th century, Alnwick has been the seat of the influential Percy family, Dukes of Northumberland.

The castle shows a pastoral face on the side furthest from the busy little town

Although Alnwick was said to be well fortified by the 12th century, it was strengthened further in the 14th century by the Percys, who rebuilt the keep and enclosed the castle inside walls with seven semi-circular towers. Sturdy gatehouses were added to both the inner and the outer walls.

After the Wars of the Roses, Alnwick began to decline. Restoration work started in the 18th century. In the 19th century it was further restored and embellished – its exterior an imposing recreation of its medieval appearance, its interior an Italian Renaissance-style treasure-house of works of art.

Open from May to September daily, except Sunday. Tel: 01665 510777.

Bamburgh is one of the most dramatically set castles in England

---
❖

BAMBURGH CASTLE
Northumberland

BAMBURGH, 16 MILES (26 KM) NORTH OF ALNWICK
❖
---

*B*amburgh's location, standing proud on a rocky promontory on the rugged Northumbrian coast, makes it one of the most spectacular of all the English castles. It is built high on a cliff, 150 feet (46m) above the North Sea. Its landward sides are protected by a forbidding display of strong walls. Bamburgh can be seen for miles, presenting a formidable obstacle to any would-be attackers.

There have been fortifications on the site for thousands of years. There was an Iron Age fort here, and the Romans, Anglo-Saxons and Vikings all left their marks. It is known that the Normans had established some kind of castle by 1095, for historical records mention that it was attacked by William II. It was also attacked by Warwick, 'The Kingmaker', during the Wars of the Roses, and much damage was done to its walls. Thereafter, it fell into disrepair, but was substantially restored during the 18th and 19th centuries.

Looking at the present day structure of Bamburgh, it is not easy to distinguish its different periods of construction. The great tower, although altered over the years, is perhaps the most dominant feature, and there are traces of the original defensive walls, although these, too, have been much restored.

Open from April to October every afternoon. Tel: 01668 214208/214515.

BARNARD CASTLE
County Durham

BARNARD CASTLE, 20 MILES (32 KM) WEST OF DARLINGTON

*F*rom a small enclosure established in the late 11th century, Barnard Castle grew to cover a site approximately 6½ acres (2.6ha). Most of this site is protected by steep cliffs, and the castle itself commands fine views across the River Tees. Sturdy walls and ditches provided additional protection.

Barnard Castle's early history revolved around its disputed ownership. It fell into Scottish hands after a successful siege by Alexander II, King of Scotland, but the powerful Prince-Bishops of Durham also claimed it as theirs. When King John of Scotland was deposed in 1296 the Prince-Bishops seized the castle, but four years later Edward I gave it to the Earl of Warwick. Richard III owned it for a short while, and his emblem – a white boar – can still be seen carved into a window.

The most imposing part of the castle is the 13th-century Round Tower, a 40 foot (12m) structure built of fine red sandstone. It is thought that an earlier tower was demolished to make way for the current one. The Round Tower has an unusual forebuilding, or porch, which gave it additional security.

Open all year daily, except Christmas and New Year. Tel: 01833 690606.

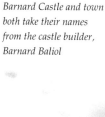
Barnard Castle and town both take their names from the castle builder, Barnard Baliol

BEESTON CASTLE
Cheshire

BEESTON, 9½ MILES (15 KM) SOUTH-EAST OF CHESTER

At first glance, Beeston's crumbling walls, perched on top of a rocky promontory, might appear to be too ruined to be of interest, but this once-powerful hilltop fortress has many features that are worth a second glance. It is steeped in history, not least as a key location in the Civil War, when the castle was besieged. Although the well continued to provide fresh water, the garrison was forced to surrender when it ran out of food. The well can still be seen, near one of the D-shaped towers in the inner bailey. It is 370 feet (113m) deep, and one of the deepest castle wells in the country.

Building work on the castle began in the 1220s, under the instructions of Ranulf, the influential Earl of Chester. In 1237 it passed to Henry III, who used it as a prison for luckless captives taken during his wars with Wales. Edward II added more walls and strengthened existing towers, and by the time of his murder in 1307, Beeston was virtually completed.

There is a legend that Richard II may have disposed of some of his treasure at Beeston Castle, but extensive searches have so far proved unsuccessful.

Open all year daily, except winter Mondays, Christmas and New Year. Tel: 01829 260464.

Beeston Castle stands dramatically on top of an isolated outcrop

Standing on the northern slopes of Wensleydale, Bolton Castle looks almost intact when seen from the valley below

---
※
BOLTON CASTLE
North Yorkshire

CASTLE BOLTON, 15 MILES (24 KM) SOUTH-WEST OF RICHMOND

※

Lord Scrope was Richard II's Chancellor – although he did not hold office for very long, for he was outspoken about the way in which the young King squandered treasury funds. Several times he refused to set his seal to some of the King's more lavish bouts of spending. Before Scrope resigned his office at Richard's Court, he was granted a licence to upgrade his manor house in Wensleydale to a castle. He hired a master mason called John Lewyn, who had also worked on the great castles of Raby and Dunstanburgh, to build him a formidable square fortress.

Bolton Castle is built in the form of a quadrangle, with strong towers at each corner. There was only one entry into the courtyard, and that was through a vaulted passage with a portcullis at each end, also protected by a guardhouse. Inside the courtyard, every door that led into the buildings had its own portcullis. The buildings themselves were constructed of local stone, although the decorative arches over some of the doors and windows were made of the more expensive freestone from a quarry a little farther away.

During the Civil War the castle was besieged for more than a year by Cromwell's troops, and finally taken in 1645.

Open from March to October daily. Tel: 01969 23981.

BROUGHAM CASTLE
Cumbria

1 MILE (1.5 KM) SOUTH-EAST OF PENRITH

Now derelict, Brougham Castle stands in a picturesque location beside the River Eamont

The restoration of Brougham, and of the nearby Appleby and Brough Castles, is chiefly the work of the immensely rich and powerful Anne Clifford, Countess of Dorset, Pembroke and Montgomery. She wanted all three of her castles to be habitable, and spent large sums of money on making them so. She died in Brougham Castle in 1678 when she was almost 90 years old.

Brougham's origins date back to the time of Henry II when – probably around 1170 – the great tower was built. It was made of sandstone rubble, with more expensive, decorative cut stone at the corners and on windows and doors. The tower had buttresses on three walls, and a forebuilding on the fourth wall. It seems that the tower was originally intended to have only three storeys, but a fourth floor was added later. This later work is of a much better quality than the original, a difference that can be clearly distinguished today. Other buildings were added to the keep, most notably in the 17th century by Anne Clifford. However, the splendid great tower remains Brougham's most impressive feature, still standing almost to its original height.

Open from April to October daily. Tel: 01768 62488.

The squat strength of Carlisle Castle, crouching on a low hill, symbolises its turbulent history

CARLISLE CASTLE
Cumbria

CARLISLE, 20 MILES (32 KM) NORTH OF PENRITH

Carlisle's location so close to the Scottish border ensured that it played an important role in British history. It was held by David I and Malcolm IV, Kings of Scotland, from 1136 until 1157, and was taken back into English hands by Henry II. Another Scottish king, William the Lion, besieged the castle from 1173 to 1174.

The first castle overlooking the River Eden was nothing more than a triangular area of land encircled by a wooden fence. It was erected by William Rufus, the son of William the Conqueror, in 1092. When William Rufus was killed in a hunting accident in the New Forest, his brother Henry became king. Henry ordered that the town of Carlisle should be protected by walls and a castle. His precautions seemed well-advised, because 14 years later King David attacked. Despite the new fortifications the castle fell to the Scots.

Although Carlisle has been greatly altered and restored through the years, there is still much of the original to see. There is a fine 14th-century gatehouse in the inner enclosure, and visitors can still admire the buttressing on some of the walls. Queen Mary's Tower now houses the Museum of the Border Regiment & King's Own Royal Border Regiment.

Open all year daily, except Christmas and New Year. Tel: 01228 591922.

CLIFFORD'S TOWER
North Yorkshire

YORK, 22 MILES (35.5 KM) EAST OF HARROGATE

The site of Clifford's Tower was the scene of one of the most bloody incidents in York's history. In 1190 the city's Jewish population was rounded up and put into the castle, which was then burned to the ground. This unpleasant episode of English history was merely one event in a whole series of anti-Jewish riots that culminated in their expulsion from the country in 1290.

A second castle was quickly built, which involved raising the mound – originally built in about 1070 from layers of clay and marl, gravel and stones, and timber – to its present height of about 60 feet (18m). The new tower did not last long, but was blown down in a gale in 1228. Henry III ordered that a third tower should be built, and during the following quarter of a century the quatrefoil shell keep was erected on top of the mound. This unusual structure, very similar to the great tower at Etampes, near Paris, was known as the King's Tower until the 16th century. Walls and towers were also built at the bottom of the mound.

Still in its dominating position atop the grass-covered mound, Clifford's Tower is a memorable landmark in this ancient city.

Open all year daily, except Christmas and New Year. Tel: 01904 646940.

The original Clifford, Roger de Clifford, was apparently hanged from the castle in chains

Dunstanburgh was besieged by Yorkists in the Wars of the Roses, but because it was not equipped to withstand cannon bombardment, it played no active part in the Civil War.

DUNSTANBURGH CASTLE
Northumberland

12 MILES (19 KM) NORTH OF ALNWICK

onely and ruined, Dunstanburgh is one of the most dramatic and atmospheric castles in Britain. Its low walls hug the rocky coastline, and only the cries of gulls and the roar of the waves disturb its peace. In order to see the castle, you must walk from the nearby village, a distance of over a mile, but the effort is well worth while, and the absence of traffic does much to enhance the feeling of timelessness of this splendid fortress.

Dunstanburgh, unlike many other castles, was not built on the site of an earlier fortress. To understand why such a grand castle was built on such a remote part of the coast, it is necessary to look at the life of the man who built it – Thomas of Lancaster, the most powerful baron in the reign of Edward II.

The earl and his King were constantly at loggerheads, especially over the favouritism shown by Edward to certain of his Court – and in particular, to Piers Gaveston. Lancaster ordered Gaveston's brutal murder, and in the turmoil that followed, the Scots seized the opportunity to begin a series of raids in northern England. Dunstanburgh was therefore built both as a stronghold against a possible Scottish invasion, and as a retreat for Lancaster from the wrath of the incensed King.

The site occupied by Dunstanburgh is large, and there would have been plenty of space for local people and their livestock to take refuge from Scottish raids within the great, thick walls that swept around the site. The sea and steep cliffs provided further protection from attack on two sides.

Lancaster's impressive gatehouse was built between 1313 and 1325, and even in its ruinous state it exudes a sense of power and impregnability. It had three floors, and all the building materials were of the finest quality.

Dunstanburgh is unusual in that it acquired a second gatehouse about 60 years later. By this time, the castle had come into the hands of another Duke of Lancaster, the powerful John of Gaunt, third son of Edward III. Active in negotiations with the Scots, he doubtless saw the need for his castle to be strengthened, and as a man of influence, he travelled with a sizeable entourage, all of whom would have required accommodation.

Open all year daily, except Christmas and New Year. Tel: 01665 576231.

Below and right, stranded on a lonely cliff-top, the ruined towers of Dunstanburgh form a dramatic silhouette against the sky

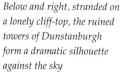

Conisbrough Castle features in Sir Walter Scott's novel 'Ivanhoe'

CONISBROUGH CASTLE
South Yorkshire

CONISBROUGH, 6 MILES (9.5 KM) SOUTH-EAST OF DONCASTER

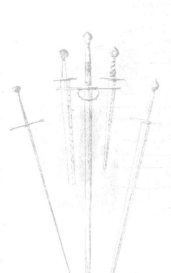

In the early 12th century, Geoffrey, the young Count of Anjou, plucked a sprig of gorse – *planta genista* – and wore it as a badge in his helmet. What began as a joke ended as a habit, earning the name 'Plantagenet' not only for himself, but also for the ruling dynasty which he founded. He married Matilda, the arrogant, embittered daughter of Henry I, and had a number of children, one of whom would later become Henry II – the first Plantagenet king of England.

Geoffrey was several years younger than his wife, and their marriage was far from happy. Like many medieval barons, he had children from other liaisons, and it was one such illegitimate child, Hamelin

Plantagenet, who built the unusually shaped tower at Conisbrough.

Hamelin began his building around 1174, and some 15 years later the keep, surrounded by walls with towers, was completed. The walls are 35 feet (11m) tall and seven feet (2.1m) thick. The tower is basically round, but with six projecting buttresses, one of which houses a six-sided chapel and some comfortable accommodation. The immensely thick walls of the 95 foot (29m) high tower contain staircases, latrines, fireplaces and hand basins. Despite this economical use of the thick walls, visitors will notice that there are very few windows or arrow loops in the tower.

Open all year daily, except Christmas and New Year. Tel: 01709 863329.

DURHAM CASTLE
County Durham

*O*n Durham city's high, rocky natural peninsula, virtually surrounded by a loop of the winding River Wear, castle and cathedral stand side by side amidst thick woodland, presenting one of the most inspiring views in the north of England. By the time of the Norman conquest, Durham was already a place of pilgrimage, and the Bishopric of Durham was a prestigious office. It was the powerful Prince-Bishops who were largely responsible for building the medieval parts of the castle that survive today.

Durham Castle began as a simple mound in around 1072, and it was not until the 12th century that a stone castle was built. This was pulled down in 1340, to be replaced by a grander castle, in keeping with the ever-rising status of the Bishops of Durham. Although this was a castle in every sense of the word, it was also an ecclesiastical palace.

Some of the earliest work that has survived includes the beautiful chapel crypt, and one of the finest Norman archways in Britain. Between 1494 and 1500, the Bishop of Durham had some enormous kitchens installed; these kitchens are still functional, providing meals for students, since the castle is now part of the University of Durham. The castle also shows signs of some Victorian remodelling.

Guided tours are available on selected afternoons. Tel: 0191 374 3863.

The castle stands in a commanding position above the city

✱
LINDISFARNE CASTLE
Northumberland

13 MILES (21 KM) SOUTH-EAST OF BERWICK-UPON-TWEED
✱

*T*wice a day, the tide covers the ancient causeway that connects Holy Island, or Lindisfarne, to the mainland. Anyone who misjudges the tide must wait until the causeway opens up again in several hours, and it is not unknown for people and vehicles to be trapped by the rising tide while halfway across.

Perhaps it was this daily encroachment by the sea that attracted the early Christians to the island, for Lindisfarne has a rich history that dates back to the saints of the 7th century. In the 11th century, the Benedictines founded a monastery here, the remains of which can still be visited.

The castle, however, is comparatively modern. It was built in the 16th century, when raids by the Scots were a serious problem, and used stones taken from the recently dissolved Benedictine monastery. However, when James I of England and VI of Scotland united the two countries, the need for border defences declined and Lindisfarne was allowed to fall into disrepair. It saw action briefly in the second Jacobite uprising, when two Jacobite supporters seized control of the little fortress and its garrison of seven men, and held it for one night.

In 1903 Lindisfarne was lovingly restored for Edward Hudson (the founder of *Country Life* magazine) by the leading country house architect Sir Edwin Lutyens. Lutyens changed very little of the structure, but used his considerable skills to convert austere stone-vaulted ammunition rooms into comfortable living quarters. The castle is a labyrinth of small tunnels and bizarrely-shaped rooms, all decorated in the style of a 17th-century Dutch mansion, with an abundance of sturdy oak furniture, brass candlesticks and attractive blue and white pottery.

Many of the bedrooms are tiny, and are dwarfed by the great four-poster beds that Lutyens chose. The many living rooms, most with splendid views out to sea or down the coast, have handsome, arched fireplaces and a wealth of nooks and crannies in which Lutyens inserted small window seats. There are three floors: the upper gallery, the upper battery, and the lower battery. Lutyens made use of these different levels to create an impression of size, so that the little stairways, numerous rooms and narrow passageways make the castle seem more extensive than it actually is.

Since 1968, this romantic Edwardian fortress has been in the care of the National Trust. Although no longer inhabited, it has been preserved as though it were, creating a comfortable air of timelessness.

Open from April to September, daily except Friday, and selected afternoons in October. Tel: 01289 89244

Below and left, Lindisfarne Castle is a ruined 16th-century fort, converted into a private home by Sir Edwin Lutyens in 1903

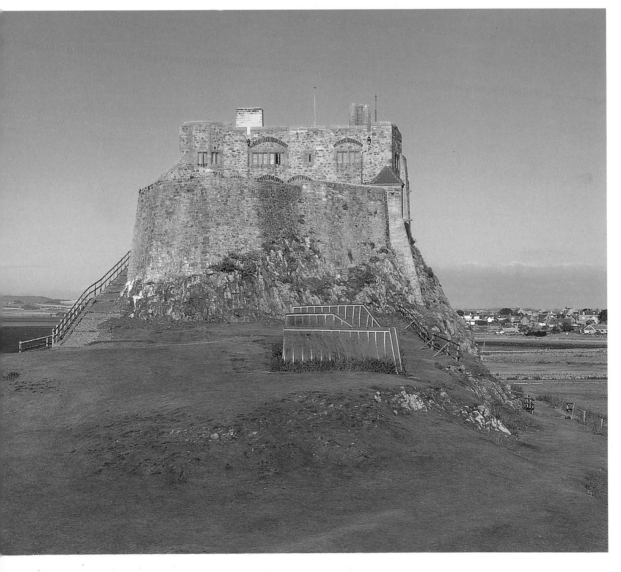

NEWCASTLE UPON TYNE CASTLE

Tyne and Wear

NEWCASTLE UPON TYNE, 9 MILES (14.5 KM) EAST OF SOUTH SHIELDS

*F*ew who travel to Newcastle by train know that the railway station lies across the site of one of the most important medieval castles in northern England. Newcastle Castle was huge, and was surrounded by great walls and defensive ditches. There were also several towers to add strength to the site, including the Black Gate, which had its own drawbridge, passage with gates, a portcullis, and a terrifying number of arrow slits.

Much of the castle has been destroyed, including the great hall, which was demolished in 1809. But one building that has survived is the splendid keep, its 12th-century walls rising tall and proud over the bustle of the modern city. It is built of sandstone, and the walls are generally between 15 and 18 feet (4.6m and 5.5m) thick and 65 feet (20m) high. There are five floors, although the upper one is mainly a wall gallery. One room contains a well, which is 100 feet (30m) deep and lined with cut stone. The basins and pipes in this room suggest that water was probably transported to other (lower) parts of the building at one time. There is also a chapel with some fine moulded arches.

Open all year, daily except Monday and Christmas, but open on Bank Holidays. Tel: 0191 232 7938.

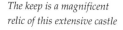

The keep is a magnificent relic of this extensive castle

NORHAM CASTLE
Northumberland

7 MILES (11 KM) SOUTH-WEST OF BERWICK-UPON-TWEED

Norham Castle has been the scene of many battles and sieges since the 12th century

Norham was so close to the Scottish border, and was besieged or captured by either the English or the Scots with such frequency, that repairs were being carried out almost constantly from the 12th to the 16th centuries. In fact, the first building, founded by Flambard, Bishop of Durham in 1120, survived only 20 years before it was destroyed by the Scots.

King James IV of Scotland and his army surrounded the castle in 1513 and bombarded it with heavy artillery, destroying parts of the newly renovated great tower. The castle garrison surrendered, just a few days before James was killed at the Scottish defeat at the Battle of Flodden Field.

Although foundations and walls of what was once a strong fortress remain, the most imposing feature at Norham is the huge rectangular keep, its thick walls still towering up to 90 feet (27m) in places. It originally had three floors (including the vaulted basement), and most of this was completed after 1158 by the Prince-Bishop of Durham, who held the castle for many years. It passed to the crown in 1173, and King John may have been responsible for the building of the Sheep Gate. In the 15th century, a further two floors were added.

Open all year daily, except Christmas and New Year. Tel: 01289 382329.

PRUDHOE CASTLE
Northumberland

PRUDHOE, 10 MILES (16 KM) WEST OF NEWCASTLE UPON TYNE

When Prudhoe's attractive square keep was raised around 1175, it was one of the first great towers to be built in Northumberland. At the same time, or perhaps slightly later, a gatehouse was added, along with stone curtain walls. However, the castle's history predates the Norman keep, for in 1173 and again in 1174, William the Lion, King of Scotland, laid siege to the early 12th-century earthworks. Although these sieges were ultimately unsuccessful, it was doubtless the threat of further Scottish attacks that prompted Henry II to grant permission for a stone castle to be built.

Prudhoe was provided with a moat and drawbridge, two barbicans and a stronger gatehouse in the 13th century. A fine vaulted basement was built under the gatehouse, and a chapel was added on the first floor. The chapel had a beautiful oriel (bay) window that is thought to be one of the earliest of its kind in any English castle.

In 1381 Prudhoe passed into the hands of the influential Percy family, who were at this time still very much rivals of the other great family in the north, the Nevilles.

Open from April to October, daily. Tel: 01661 33459.

Few visitors stop at Prudhoe today, but it is a fine castle, and well worth a detour

RICHMOND CASTLE
North Yorkshire

RICHMOND, 4 MILES (6.5 KM) SOUTH-WEST OF SCOTCH CORNER

Never seriously threatened, Richmond has now surrendered itself gracefully to time

Commanding a powerful position on the banks of the River Swale, this mighty fortress was never put to the test, for Richmond has never seen military action. Its location is superb, with steep cliffs protecting one side, and thick walls defending the other sides.

The Normans started constructing a castle here in the 1080s, and it is thought that Scolland's Hall, a fine two-storeyed hall with typical round-headed windows, is one of the earliest stone-built halls in England. The towers at Richmond have romantic names: Robin Hood Tower, now in ruins, is said to have been the prison of William the Lion, King of Scotland; the Gold Hole Tower may have a poetic ring to its name, but it was actually the latrine tower, complete with pits at its base, spanned by an interesting 11th-century arch. By far the largest building of the entire complex is the keep. It started life as a gatehouse in the 11th century, but in the mid 12th century it was extended upwards to a height of 100 feet (30m). Straight flights of stairs ran between the floors, rather than the traditional spiral stairways.

Open all year daily, except Christmas and New Year. Tel: 01748 822133.

Scarborough Castle is a formidable sight even in its ruinous state today

---
❊
SCARBOROUGH CASTLE
North Yorkshire

SCARBOROUGH, 44 MILES (70.5 KM) NORTH-EAST OF YORK
❊

Unlike most medieval castles, Scarborough saw action in World War I, when shells from German battleships damaged its walls. Historical records indicate that this was by no means the first time that the castle had come under attack, and several English kings received bills for repairs, from Henry II to James I.

The rocky headland on which the castle was built had been an important site for hundreds of years before the Normans came, the cliffs providing a natural defence which was further strengthened by curtain walls. The keep, now in ruins, was built by Henry II on the site of an earlier tower. It was originally 100 feet (30m) high, and had walls that were up to 12 feet (3.7m) thick. There was also a forebuilding that has not survived.

Scarborough was also attacked in 1536 during the 'Pilgrimage of Grace', a rebellion against Henry VIII which protested against issues such as the Dissolution of the Monasteries, the Reformation and a whole host of economic grievances. The rebellion, mainly in the north, was led by Robert Ashe. Henry VIII agreed to listen to the complaints of the leaders, but as soon as the rebels began to disband, he had 230 of them, including Ashe, executed.

Open all year daily, except Christmas and New Year. Tel: 01723 372451.

SKIPTON CASTLE
North Yorkshire

SKIPTON, 9 MILES (14.5 KM) NORTH-WEST OF KEIGHLEY

The yew tree in Skipton Castle's conduit court was planted by Lady Anne Clifford in the 17th century

*T*wo cannon stand on either side of the stalwart doors of Skipton Castle's powerful medieval gatehouse. Although the castle dates from much earlier, it is strongly associated with the Civil War, when the busy market town and the castle came under heavy attack from cannon such as these. The castle was so badly damaged that by the time the troops had left, it was almost totally destroyed, and the gatehouse that stands proudly at the head of the main street today is the result of some painstaking restoration work.

Skipton Castle is the result of several building phases. The earliest stonework was raised during the 12th century on the site of an earlier castle. More towers and some sturdy walls were added in the 13th and 14th centuries. Some of these walls were 12 feet (3.7m) thick in places, and so it is not surprising that Skipton was able to hold out against the siege of the Civil War for so long. There was a moat here, too, although this has long since disappeared.

Open all year daily, except Christmas Day. Tel: 01756 79244.

WARKWORTH CASTLE
Northumberland

WARKWORTH, 10 MILES (16 KM) SOUTH-EAST OF ALNWICK

Shakespeare used Warkworth Castle as the scene of the Percys' treacherous rebellion against Henry IV in *Richard II*, describing it as 'this worm-eaten hold of ragged stone'. Although Warkworth would have been a formidable fortress in Hotspur's lifetime, when Shakespeare wrote the play in the late 16th century, the castle was already sadly neglected.

Below and right, the keep and the gatehouse dominate the crumbling walls of Warkworth Castle

When William the Lion, King of Scotland, seized Warkworth in 1173, it was widely thought that this had been possible because the castle was 'feeble in wall and earthwork'. Subsequent owners apparently decided that this description should not be applied to Warkworth a second time, for the castle that can be seen today is one of the most powerful fortresses in northern England.

The unusually shaped keep was raised by the Earl of Northumberland in around 1390. It is basically square, but has towers projecting from each of its four sides. One of these towers contained an elegant chapel, and there were comfortable living quarters in some of the others. Rainwater was collected on the roof and channelled to holding tanks in the basement, permit-ting a constant supply of clean water to many of the basins and latrines – a great luxury in a medieval castle. The Earl, doubtless wishing his castle to reflect his status as one of the most powerful noblemen in the country, ordered that the keep should contain separate living quarters to divide him and his family from the rest of the garrison. It was probably this same earl who ordered the building of what would have been a fine chapel in the castle courtyard. Although the foundations of this church can still be seen, the building was never actually completed.

The Earl and his famous son, Hotspur, are perhaps the most renowned residents of the castle, for it was they who fought so hard to put Henry IV on the throne in 1399, and to force the rightful king, Richard II, to

abdicate. Four years later, these two men fought equally hard to wrest the crown from Henry once more. The King promptly marched to Warkworth and blasted its walls with cannon-fire until the castle surrendered.

The King then gave Warkworth to his brother, later the Duke of Bedford, although it was restored to Hotspur's son in 1416. The Percys' political favour continued to wax and wane during the 15th century, and in 1572 Sir Thomas Percy was executed for his part in a plot against Elizabeth I. With his death, this great fortress began to decline in importance and gradually fell into ruins.

Abutting onto the Percys' keep were walls that formed a large enclosure containing several buildings, now mostly ruins, although the Lion Tower (named after the Percy lion) and the Grey Mare's Tail Tower, with its massive fan-tailed crossbow loops, can still be seen.

Open all year daily, except Christmas and New Year. Tel: 01665 711423.

ARDVRECK CASTLE
Highland

26 MILES (41.5 KM) NORTH-EAST OF ULLAPOOL

When Civil War broke out in England in 1642, Scotland was inevitably drawn into the conflict. Two of the main protagonists in the north were Archibald Campbell, Marquess of Argyll, and James Graham, Marquess of Montrose. Montrose remained loyal to the King, while Argyll declared for Parliament. After the execution of Charles I in 1649, Montrose fled the country, but returned a year later. He was captured by the Laird of Assynt, who held him in Ardvreck Castle until he could be safely handed over to Cromwell's forces. Montrose was hastily executed in the same year, while his rival, Argyll, was executed after the Restoration of the monarchy in 1661.

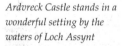
Ardvreck Castle stands in a wonderful setting by the waters of Loch Assynt

The small 16th-century tower house is now a ruin, perched on a rocky peninsula that juts out into Loch Assynt. It was a simple structure – rectangular, with a staircase turret on the south-east corner. The basement had three chambers with vaulted roofs. One of the chambers is little more than a passage, but the gun loops pierced in its outer wall suggests that it could have been used to defend the castle. When observing Ardvreck Castle, visitors may notice some other ruins nearby. These are the remains of Edderchalder House, a fine 17th-century mansion.

The castle can be seen from the A837, and is best admired from a distance – the ruins are in a dangerous condition.

BLAIR CASTLE
Tayside

BLAIR ATHOLL, 8 MILES (13 KM) FROM PITLOCHRY

Blair, a story-book castle, is set among forested hills above the River Garry

*I*n 1269 affairs of state forced David, Earl of Atholl, to spend a considerable amount of time in England. While he was away, his neighbour, John Comyn, began to build a castle on Atholl's land, causing Atholl to complain to King Alexander III. This early tower is now incorporated into a much bigger castle, but is still called Cummings (or Comyn's) Tower.

The Earls and Dukes of Atholl were prominent men in Scottish history. The simple tower house was extended and rebuilt over the centuries according to the needs of its different owners. In the English Civil War, Blair, then a fortress with good defences, was captured by Cromwell's forces. In 1745 it was besieged by the Jacobites, in what was probably the last siege to take place in Britain.

Most of the castle as it is seen today dates from the 18th century. It is a splendid palace, its gleaming white walls contrasting starkly with the rich woodland in which it stands. Many richly furnished rooms are open to the public, and some contain objects of great historical significance, including two cannon from an Armada galleon and an original copy of the National Covenant of 1638.

Open from April to October daily. Tel: 01796 481207.

Blair's Private Army

When Queen Victoria came to stay at Blair Castle in 1844, some 200 Athollmen formed a royal bodyguard, so enchanting the young Queen that she presented them with their colours in the following year. As the only private army in the country, the Atholl Highlanders, still recruited largely from the estate, exist today as a ceremonial private bodyguard.

BOTHWELL CASTLE
Strathclyde

BOTHWELL, 7½ MILES (12 KM) SOUTH-EAST OF GLASGOW

*O*n 29 August 1301, 30 wagons began a cumbersome two-day journey from Glasgow to the mighty fortress at Bothwell. Carried on these wagons were the parts for an enormous siege tower that had been commissioned by Edward I, the 'Hammer of the Scots', from the men of Glasgow. When the siege tower, or 'bellfry' as contemporary accounts call it, was reconstructed from its many sections, it stood higher than the castle walls. It was basically a vast platform on wheels, with a drawbridge at the top, that could be pushed close to the walls so that besiegers could storm the castle. Faced with this weapon, Bothwell fell to Edward's army within just a few days.

Bothwell Castle was one of the most important military strongholds in Scotland. Its great tower was built in the 1270s, and was a powerful structure with walls 80 feet (24 m) high and 15 feet (4.6 m) thick. Later, thick walls and a powerful gatehouse were added.

Because Bothwell was so prominent in the Scottish struggle for independence, it was attacked and fell many times during the 13th and 14th centuries. Each time damage was done and repairs were made, and so it can be difficult to date some of the surviving ruins. Several great towers and walls still jut defiantly into the air, giving the derelict castle an undeniable air of power.

Open all year, daily except winter Fridays, Christmas and New Year. Tel: 0131 244 3101.

Parts of Bothwell have survived since the 13th century

❄
BRODICK CASTLE
Arran, Strathclyde

2 MILES (3 KM) FROM BRODICK PIER HEAD
❄

For generations Brodick Castle was the heart of the Isle of Arran estate which belonged to the Dukes of Hamilton

After Robert the Bruce's defeat at Methven in 1306, he fled to Brodick Castle on the Isle of Arran. It was here that he is supposed to have waited for the beacon to be lit on the mainland, telling him the time was ripe to begin afresh his war with the English King Edward I. Within a year, Edward was dead and Bruce was establishing himself as King of Scotland.

Nowadays, little remains of the 14th-century castle which, according to contemporary accounts, was 'levelled to the ground' in 1455 by the Earl of Ross. It was rebuilt, but in 1544 the Earl of Lennox destroyed it, acting on the orders of Henry VIII. The castle was repaired again in the 1630s so that it could be garrisoned for Charles I, but these buildings were largely swept away for the Scots baronial mansion that was designed by James Gillespie Graham in the 19th century.

The mansion is an elegant red sandstone building, displaying clusters of chimneys, gables and towers, and nestling comfortably in its attractive gardens. A number of rooms are open, displaying a diverse collection of sporting trophies and some excellent paintings. Famous rhododendron gardens and extensive woodlands are also to be found on the estate.

Open at Easter, then May to September afternoons; also at weekends in April and October. Tel: 01770 302202.

CAERLAVEROCK CASTLE
Dumfries and Galloway

CAERLAVEROCK, 12 MILES (19 KM) SOUTH-EAST OF DUMFRIES

*T*he imposing gatehouse at Caerlaverock Castle is so similar to those designed by Edward I's master castle-builder, James of St George, that it is often suggested that this was an English, rather than a Scottish, fortress. The high walls, with their massive round towers, two moats and high ramparts, are very similar to the concentric castles built by Edward in Wales, such as Beaumaris and Harlech; but, unlike any other castle in Britain, Caerlaverock is triangular. It has three walls, two protected by an arm of the sea that swings out round the back of the castle, and the third by moats, earthworks, and the great gatehouse.

Caerlaverock was built in the late 13th century, and exchanged hands several times when Edward invaded Scotland. Edward laid siege to it in 1300, after which it was besieged another four times during its eventful history. Often, if the Scots took a castle but were unable to hold it, they would destroy it so that the English could not use it. This happened to Caerlaverock in 1312, and it was almost completely rebuilt in the 15th century. Rebuilding followed the previous plan, although gun ports were added, and the great gatehouse was strengthened to withstand cannonfire.

Open all year, daily except Christmas and New Year. Tel: 0131 244 3101.

The Renaissance walls and carved stone panels still remain at Caerlaverock

CENTRAL *CASTLE CAMPBELL* 121

CASTLE CAMPBELL
Central

DOLLAR, 10 MILES (16 KM) EAST OF STIRLING

The ruins of Castle Campbell loom romantically above some of Scotland's finest countryside

The original name of this stronghold was 'the Castle of Gloume', but the first Earl of Argyll disliked the name and changed it by an Act of Parliament in 1489 to the less dismal Castle Campbell. The castle stands on a rocky spur of land between two streams, rather mournfully named the Burn of Care and the Burn of Sorrow.

It is not known exactly when the first castle was raised here, but the earliest surviving building dates to the end of the 15th century. This fine tower is in an excellent state of preservation, and stands about 60 feet (18m) high to its parapets. It has four storeys, three of which have handsome vaulted ceilings, and there was a pit prison in the basement. During the 16th century the simple tower house was extended to form a quadrangle, although the castle's position on a rocky knoll of land meant that further development was restricted.

During the English Civil War, Castle Campbell's owner, the Earl of Argyll, sided firmly with Cromwell. In 1654 Castle Campbell was burned by Royalists, and in 1661 Argyll was executed. Since then, much of the castle has remained derelict, although the splendid tower house and the east wing were used as a residence by the Argylls until the early 19th century.

Open all year daily in summer, most days in winter. Tel: 0131-244 3101.

Robert the Bruce and Scottish Independence

*I*n the late 13th century, Edward I, one of England's greatest warrior kings, attempted to thoroughly subjugate the peoples on the borders of his kingdom. In 1282 Llywelyn the Last, the final true Welsh Prince of Wales, was killed in an ambush, and Edward quickly pressed home his advantage by building castles in north Wales, ensuring the continued domination of that nation. The subjugation of Scotland, however, did not prove so straightforward.

When King Alexander III of Scotland died in 1286, leaving no clear heir to the throne, Edward capitalised on the ensuing division between the Balliol and Bruce families in an attempt to bring Scotland under English control. But he reckoned without William Wallace, a knight who inspired the people of Scotland to revolt against Edward's control. In 1297 Wallace led a great army against Edward's troops at Stirling Bridge and routed them. In 1303 Edward gave Scotland his full attention, marching to Stirling to retake the castle. Wallace was executed by Edward in 1305, and from this time, Robert the Bruce became the leader in the struggle for Scottish independence.

Edward died in 1307, but his aggressive policies in Scotland were carried on (less successfully) by his son, Edward II. In the following decade, Scottish castles changed hands with bewildering rapidity. Although Bruce had suffered a humiliating defeat at the Battle of Methven in 1306, his fortunes changed in 1307 and he became one of Scotland's most dynamic kings, taking back from the English all the castles Edward had won.

Stirling was, perhaps, the castle that faced the greatest number of changes – Edward took it in 1296 and Wallace took it back in 1297; Edward captured it in 1298 and Wallace recaptured it in

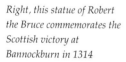

Right, this statue of Robert the Bruce commemorates the Scottish victory at Bannockburn in 1314

1299, holding it until Edward took it back in 1304. It then remained in English hands until the great Scottish victory at Bannockburn delivered it back to Bruce in 1314. Many castles suffered a similar fate – Bothwell, Caerlaverock, Dirleton, Edinburgh, Dunstaffnage, Hermitage, Kildrummy, Roxburgh and Urquhart all had English and Scottish occupying forces in them at least twice during the period from 1297 and 1314.

When Wallace or Bruce seized a castle from the English, they were often painfully aware that their hold would be temporary, and would 'slight' the building to prevent any future use as an English garrison. Dirleton and Roxburgh suffered this fate. Bruce also slighted Edinburgh, though the damage did not deter the English king, who, within a few years, had repaired it and had even planted a garden in anticipation of a long stay.

Castles survived the roller-coaster fortunes of the Wars of Independence to varying degrees. Some, like Stirling and Edinburgh, continued to be of service to the Scottish nation, while others gradually fell into disrepair.

Above, Stirling Castle today has adapted gracefully to a more peaceful invasion

CAWDOR CASTLE
Highland

CAWDOR, 6 MILES (10 KM) SOUTH-WEST OF NAIRN

Cawdor Castle has had a violent history. It was home to the Thanes of Cawdor, who played an active role in local Scottish politics throughout the centuries, but the 9th Thane was branded on the hip with a hot key as a child, and both the 4th and the 11th Thanes were murdered.

Cawdor is also associated with Macbeth's murder of King Duncan, but as Macbeth lived during the 11th century, and Cawdor was not built until the 14th century, the link between Duncan's bloody murder and Cawdor Castle may be poetic licence.

Nevertheless, the appearance of the austere tower and battlements make it easy to imagine why Shakespeare chose it as the location for his grim tale of madness and regicide. The keep dates from the 15th century, and is a forbidding grey tower with walls 11 feet (3.4 m) thick in places, once surrounded by a deep ditch. The later buildings sprout an attractive array of steep-sided roofs, crow-stepped gables, and small turrets dating from the 17th and 19th centuries. Inside, visitors can explore parts of the keep and rooms in the later buildings. There is a fine 17th-century kitchen displaying an array of antique household utensils, and bedrooms containing an elegant Georgian bed and an exquisite Flemish tapestry.

Open daily from May to October. Tel: 01667 404615.

The castle is the ancient seat of the Thanes of Cawdor

CLAYPOTTS CASTLE
Tayside

ABOUT 2 MILES (3 KM) EAST OF DUNDEE

Standing on the fringes of a modern housing estate, Claypotts is one of the finest and most complete examples of a Scottish 'Z-plan' tower house – quite literally, a tower that was built in the shape of a Z. Other popular ground plans of 16th-century Scottish domestic architecture include E-plans, L-plans, and even Y-plans.

Claypotts comprises a square tower, with two round towers diagonally opposite each other, so that one tower adjoins the north-east corner, and the other adjoins the south-west corner. This shape was practical, because it allowed defenders to fire their weapons across all the faces of the main building, making it impossible for attackers to approach too closely without exposing themselves to gunfire. In order to ensure that every possible angle was covered by protective fire, a gun loop was even put in the back of the kitchen fireplace. Although this has been blocked up, it can still be clearly seen.

The arrangement of the three linked towers provided 16 rooms on four floors. The ground floor was used for storerooms and the kitchen, while the upper floors would have provided lavish accommodation for the Laird, his family, and their guests.

Open from April to September, daily. Tel: 0131-244 3101.

Claypotts Castle is an excellent example of a Z-plan tower house

Craigeivar Castle is still as proud and imposing as ever

CRAIGIEVAR CASTLE
Grampian

7 MILES (11 KM) SOUTH OF ALFORD

Standing amid attractive woodland, and built of a delicate rose-pink granite, Craigievar is one of the most romantic of the 17th-century Scottish tower houses. Although it is perhaps one of the most lavish and ornate, it was also one of the last of its kind to be built. Within two decades of its completion the Civil War broke out in England, and many castles and fortified houses came under devastating bombardment from cannon. Since it was no longer possible to build a house that could withstand such fire-power indefinitely, fortresses became obsolete, and in their places came the elegant Classical-style mansions and townhouses of the 18th century.

No expense was spared by the wealthy merchant, Sir William Forbes, who built Craigievar in the 1620s. It was he who ordered the decorative turrets that adorn each corner and the elegant carvings high up on the walls. Inside the castle are more reminders of Forbes' wealth. Many rooms have retained their impressive Renaissance plaster ceilings, and the elegant hall has arcaded panelling with a royal coat of arms over the granite fireplace. This magical L-plan castle is now owned by the National Trust for Scotland, and nearly all the rooms are open to visitors.

Open from May to September, daily. Tel: 01339 883635.

CRAIGMILLAR CASTLE
Lothian

2½ MILES (4 KM) SOUTH-EAST OF EDINBURGH

Buildings from four different periods make up the splendid ruins at Craigmillar. A simple L-plan tower house was built here in the late 14th century, of red-grey sandstone. In the 1420s, this sturdy tower was fortified by the addition of a 28 foot (8.5 m) wall with round towers at the corners, which ran all the way around it. Another set of walls and other buildings were added in the 16th and 17th centuries, including a chapel and kitchens, the remains of which can still be seen.

Although Craigmillar is a good example of a late medieval fortress, it is perhaps better known for its role in history. The first significant bloody act at Craigmillar was the murder of the Earl of Mar by a jealous brother in 1477. It was attacked and seriously damaged by the Earl of Hereford for Henry VIII in 1544, but was sufficiently repaired for Mary, Queen of Scots to retreat there following the murder of a favourite secretary in 1566. While Mary grieved for her loss, her noblemen plotted revenge. It is not known whether Mary was a party to the plot, but a pact was signed that resulted in the murder of Mary's estranged husband, Lord Darnley. While convalescing from a disease, his house was blown up. When his body was recovered, it was found that Darnley had been strangled before the explosion.

Open all year daily except winter Fridays. Tel: 0131-244 3101.

Craigmillar is linked to a notorious incident in the life of Mary, Queen of Scots

Pepper-pot towers cling to the 16th-century Crathes Castle

CRATHES CASTLE
Grampian

CRATHES, 3 MILES (5 KM) EAST OF BANCHORY

Crathes Castle is said to have a ghost that haunts one of its rooms. One version of the story is that the illegitimate child of a lady was murdered and buried under the hearth in the Green Room. It is said that moans and wails are sometimes heard echoing through Crathes' lonely halls, and that a mysterious green light has been seen by some visitors to the castle. Whether or not the story is true, a great deal more is on offer here.

Crathes was built in the 1550s for the wealthy Burnett family, and when the splendid multi-storeyed building proved too small for Thomas Burnett and his 21 children, some time in the early 18th century, he set about enlarging and restoring the castle. The outcome was the beginnings of the stately gardens that still surround the house, and an elegant building known as the Queen Anne Wing. Unfortunately, this was gutted in a serious fire in 1966, although the original L-plan tower escaped serious harm.

The building has been restored by the National Trust `for Scotland. Crathes is in the same mould as Glamis and Craigievar, harled with delicately shaded, rose granite, and capped with attractive clusters of turrets and chimneys.

Open daily, from April to October. Tel: 01330 844525.

DIRLETON CASTLE
Lothian

DIRLETON, 11 MILES (17.5 KM) NORTH-EAST OF EDINBURGH

This sturdy castle was raised in the 13th century, probably on the remains of an earlier fortress. The principal building was the impressive three-storeyed round keep or 'drum' tower, supported by a complex arrangement of other towers and walls. In the 14th and 15th centuries the castle was considerably enlarged, to include a chapel with a prison beneath, and a pit-prison hewn from the rock below that. Although a ruin, Dirleton still presents an imposing face to the world and crossing the modern wooden footbridge to the great gatehouse, it is easy to appreciate the difficulties faced by any would-be attacker.

Dorothea, wife of the rebellious Earl of Gowrie, was probably one of the saddest residents of Dirleton Castle. Her husband was executed in 1585 after a plot to seize Stirling Castle was discovered, and all his lands and castles were taken by King James VI, leaving Dorothea and her 15 children poverty-stricken. The king granted Dirleton Castle to Gowrie's great rival, the Earl of Arran, who kept it until the castle and its lands were restored to Dorothea almost two years later. Then, in 1600, two of her sons were involved in the mysterious 'Gowrie Conspiracy', when it was alleged that they tried to kill the King. Although the maiming of the corpses of Dorothea's sons was very public, details of the entire affair remained secret.

Open all year daily, except Christmas and New Year. Tel: 0131-244 3101.

Dirleton is built on a rock outcrop, surrounded by the remains of a moat

DUNNOTTAR CASTLE
Grampian

1 MILE (1.6 KM) SOUTH-EAST OF STONEHAVEN

O n the rugged coastline south of Aberdeen a great stack of rock projects into the stormy North Sea, topped by a jumbled collection of buildings spanning several centuries. Joined to the land by a narrow, crumbling neck of rock, great cliffs protect this natural fortress on all sides, while a thick wall and a gatehouse protect the castle entrance.

The first castle on the site was constructed in the 12th century, but virtually nothing remains of this early building. In the 14th century an L-plan tower house was built by William Keith, the Marischal of Scotland. This building dominates the rest of the castle, its 50 foot (15 m) walls still in good repair, although it is roofless.

More buildings were raised in the 16th century, forming a handsome quadrangular courtyard. Although the emphasis was on comfort, rather than on defence, the castle was equipped with gun ports as a safeguard against possible attack. These were used twice in the Civil War when the castle came under siege, first by the Royalists, and then by Cromwell.

In a dark episode in the castle's history, it was used as a prison for 167 Scottish Presbyterians. These people were crammed into a long, narrow chamber known as the Whigs Vault, and conditions were so appalling that many of them died.

Open all year daily, except winter weekends. Tel: 01569 762173.

Dunnottar Castle squats on top of a vast flat-topped rock, 160ft above the sea

Dunskey, lying just south of Portpatrick, occupies a spectacular coastal location

DUNSKEY CASTLE
Dumfries and Galloway

6 MILES (10 KM) SOUTH-WEST OF STRANRAER

*L*ittle is known of this ruined tower house standing on a rocky peninsula that juts out into the sea. A castle is mentioned in records dating to 1330, but was burned down early in the 15th century. A new tower was raised by William Adair of Kinhilt, but this was deserted in the middle of the 17th century, and little more than a ruin by 1684.

Dunskey is a simple L-plan tower house, with cellars, a ground floor and a first floor. Walls were built around the small peninsula, so that the castle would have been surrounded by two lines of defence: firstly the sea and ditches hewn from the rock, and secondly, the walls. Virtually nothing remains of these walls, although there are traces of other buildings in what would have been the courtyard.

It is likely that Dunskey Castle would once have been a fine, proud house. The windows and doors were once decorated with dressed stones, but these, being expensive and much in demand for building, have been stripped away over the centuries by local looters. It is the absence of these stones that gives the roofless walls of Dunskey Castle their forlorn, rugged appearance.

Open access at any reasonable time.

DUNTULM CASTLE
Isle of Skye

DUNTULM, 24 MILES (38.5 KM) NORTH OF PORTREE

This stronghold of the island clan of MacDonald stands in a commanding position overlooking a natural harbour at the extreme northern end of Skye. The rectangular tower dates from the 15th century, but a smaller tower was added in the 17th century, when the little fortress was at the height of its glory. Contemporary accounts tell of the lavish hospitality that could be enjoyed at the fine MacDonald house at Duntulm, and soil was imported from seven different countries to make the castle gardens fertile.

Several legends are attached to these atmospheric ruins. One is that the baby son of the clan chief was being dangled from a window by his nurse to see a passing ship, when she inadvertently dropped him. The chief was reported to have quit Duntulm immediately before any further misfortunes should fall on him.

A different tale involves another chief and his heir, Hugh. The story goes that Hugh was keen to inherit sooner, rather than later, and so arranged for his kinsman's murder. In an act of appalling incompetence, Hugh misaddressed his letters, sending to the chief, not the invitation to dine, but instructions to the hired killer outlining how the foul deed was to be done. Hugh was arrested and incarcerated in Duntulm's vaults with salt beef and nothing to drink. It is said that many years later a skeleton was unearthed, still clutching an empty water pitcher.

Open access at any reasonable time.

Little remains today of this former MacDonald stronghold

DUNVEGAN CASTLE
Isle of Skye

DUNVEGAN, 23 MILES (37 KM) WEST OF PORTREE

Dunvegan Castle has been the home of the MacLeod family for nearly 800 years

The story of Dunvegan Castle and its owners, the MacLeods, stretches back to the 13th century. In 1237 Leod, a son of the King of the Isle of Man and the North Isles, inherited the island of Lewis and Harris, and part of Skye. When Viking claims to the Scottish islands were finally crushed, Leod controlled a good portion of the Hebrides. He chose the rocky peninsula jutting out into the sea at Dunvegan on which to establish his fortress and headquarters. Dunvegan has remained the home of the MacLeods (meaning 'son of Leod') ever since.

Leod died in 1280, but before his death a thick wall had been built around the site, leaving only a small sea gate, through which supplies could be brought to the castle in times of siege. Between 1340 and 1360, a keep was added, which contained kitchens and a dungeon. The 'Fairy Tower' was built around 1500, while further improvements were made in the 17th century.

The entire castle was reconstructed in the 19th century, complete with noble battlements and little corner turrets, and is an impressive sight, whether approached from land or sea.

Open April to October daily. Tel: 0147022 206.

One of Dunvegan's most curious treasures is the fabled fairy flag. Modern tests have shown that this yellow silk banner dates to between AD400 and AD700, but how it came to be in the possession of the MacLeods is a mystery. There are many local legends to explain: one story tells of how it was presented to a crusader MacLeod in Palestine, while other legends insist that it was given to the family by fairies.

Cromwell bombarded the castle for three months in 1650, and it came under heavy attack by the forces of William of Orange in 1689.

EDINBURGH CASTLE
Lothian

EDINBURGH

There was no capital city of Scotland, as such, until the end of the Middle Ages. Before that, Scotland's capital was wherever the king and his court happened to be. But the magnificent fortress squatting firmly on its plug of rock was a great favourite with Scottish kings, and has played a vital role in history on many occasions. It changed hands several times when the Scots were fighting for independence from England under Robert the Bruce, and became a royal residence under the Stuart kings.

Today, it is a museum – it houses the Scottish National War Memorial and the Scottish crown jewels – and is the venue for the spectacular annual Edinburgh Military Tattoo. It still dominates the ancient city from its rocky pinnacle, and even though it has been battered and bruised through the centuries, remains one of the most impressive and best-known castles in the world.

The origins of Edinburgh Castle are shrouded in mystery. Although the great rock on which the castle stands would probably have attracted earlier strongholds, there is no archaeological evidence to prove the site was used earlier than the 11th century. Malcolm III, before his death in 1093, raised a wooden fortress here and his son, David I, built a church to the memory of his mother in the 1120s. This tiny chapel is the oldest surviving building in the castle. Thereafter, Edinburgh became an important gamepiece in the struggles between Edward I and

Below and right, Edinburgh Castle, at the heart of this great city, is one of the most famous in the world

Robert the Bruce in the late 13th century. Edward seized it in 1296, bombarding it with huge boulders from his great war machines. The garrison surrendered after only eight days, and Edward installed 350 of his own soldiers to hold it securely.

In 1313 the Earl of Moray, acting for Bruce, scaled the daunting cliffs with only 30 men and routed the English. Bruce then ordered that the castle be utterly destroyed, so that it could never again be used by Edward's forces. He underestimated Edward's tenacity, for a few years later Edward retook the site, and set about repairing the damage, even planting gardens and orchards in anticipation of a lengthy stay. But the Scots were undeterred, and in 1341 a small party of Scottish soldiers disguised themselves as merchants and quickly ambushed the startled garrison.

The vast sprawl of the castle contains buildings from many centuries. The fine half-moon battery and portcullis gate date from the 1570s, while the splendid Great Hall and the handsome palace were built for James IV in the early 16th century.

Open all year, daily. Tel: 0131-244 3101.

EDZELL CASTLE
Tayside

EDZELL, 8 MILES (13 KM) NORTH OF BRECHIN

The most remarkable feature of this sturdy little fortified tower house is its unusual gardens, complete with bath house and summer house. In 1604 a walled enclosure was added onto the already existing tower house and courtyard, designed to surround one of the most elegant and notable gardens of any castle in western Europe. The garden walls are a triumph in themselves: they have been divided into sections, and are richly adorned with carvings and sculpted panels. Exquisite in their detail, the carvings embrace several themes: the first set depicts a number of planetary deities, including Mars, Jupiter, Venus, and Saturn; the second represents 'the liberal arts'. In medieval learning, the three basic subjects were grammar, rhetoric and logic, while arithmetic, music, geometry and astronomy were the more advanced topics, and each of these is illustrated by seated figures busily practising their art.

The tower house was built in the 15th century as a home for the Lindsay family. Other buildings arranged around a courtyard were added in the 16th century. Edzell saw little military action, although it was occupied by Cromwell's troops in 1651, and was badly damaged in the second Jacobite Uprising in 1747. Today, the tower remains the most complete section, along with the quaint summer house in the south-east corner of the garden.

Open all year daily, except winter Fridays and Christmas. Tel: 0131-244 3101.

Delightful gardens surround this old tower house

The beautiful Eilean Donan Castle stands guard on a promontory where three lochs meet

EILEEN DONAN CASTLE
Highland

DORNIE, 8 MILES (12.9 KM) EAST OF KYLE OF LOCHALSH

Dwarfed by the brooding hills surrounding Loch Duich, the castle of Eilean Donan stands picturesquely on its rocky island. A fortress was built here in 1220 by Alexander II to protect himself against raids by Vikings. During the Jacobite Rebellion the Macraes opted to support the Old Pretender and garrisoned a small force of Spanish soldiers in the castle. In 1719 the guns of an English man-of-war pounded the castle to pieces.

It remained in ruins until 1912, when Colonel John Macrae decided to restore his ancestral home. Paying great attention to detail, the lakeside castle was lovingly rebuilt, along with an arched bridge that affords easier access to the castle than the ancient Macraes would have known.

Some rooms in the castle are open to visitors, all furnished in the style of the home of a country laird. There are fine collections of pistols and powder horns, and, although it is mostly a 20th-century restoration, it allows the imagination to return to the time when it was owned by the wild Macraes. A fearsome clan, they relished the displaying of the heads of their enemies from the battlements, and local legends tell how, on one occasion, they defended the castle successfully when outnumbered by their attackers 400-to-one.

Open April to September daily. Tel: 0159985 202.

CASTLE FRASER
Grampian

SAUCHEN, 16 MILES (26 KM) WEST OF ABERDEEN

*C*astle Fraser is vast. While visitors are treated to a tour that extends from the ground floor to the roof of the elegant 15th-century tower house, the two Jacobean wings that stretch out on either side of the original tower to form a courtyard are mostly closed to the public. Even so, the tower house itself contains such an extraordinary wealth of treasures, not only in terms of displays, but also architecturally, that no one will leave Castle Fraser feeling cheated.

Among the most intriguing items in the exhibition of Fraser family history, in the fine library at the top of the house, are two bullets and a wooden leg. These date from the Peninsular War of 1812, in which Colonel Charles Mackenzie Fraser lost his leg. One of the bullets is labelled 'head' and the other 'leg'.

Another curious feature is the 'luggie', or secret listening point between the hall and the chamber above. This was a small cubby-hole that was dug into the thickness of the wall, and concealed behind a window shutter. Eavesdroppers could remove the stone slab, slip into the cubby-hole, and listen to what was said in the hall below.

Open during April and October at weekends, and daily from May to September. Tel: 013303 463.

The pleasing old tower house of Castle Fraser

GLAMIS CASTLE
Tayside

GLAMIS, 12 MILES (19 KM) NORTH OF DUNDEE

A magnificent and mysterious castle, Glamis is the family home of the Queen Mother, and is the birthplace of Princess Margaret

Legends and myths about Glamis Castle are plentiful. King Malcolm II is said to have been murdered here in the 11th century; Lady Janet Douglas, the widow of the Earl of Glamis, was burned at the stake as a witch by James V in 1540; and there is said to be a secret room where one lord of Glamis played cards with the devil. It is difficult to associate such dark tales with the splendid dark red castle, with its ornate turrets and chimneys.

There was probably a castle at Glamis in the early 14th century, but it was not until after 1376 that the L-plan tower house was built by John Lyon on land presented to him by King Robert II. The Lyon family, now Earls of Strathmore and Kinghorne, have owned the castle ever since.

If Glamis today looks more like a French château than a medieval fortress, then that is because it was extensively restored and developed in the 17th and 18th centuries. The original tower house, although strengthened, heightened, and re-roofed, remains the central part of this rambling palace. Tours of the house range from the medieval hall to the 17th-century chapel, and include is the small suite of rooms used by George VI and his queen.

Open Easter weekend, then from May to September daily except Sunday; by appointment in winter. Tel: 01307 840242/3.

Glamis was one of the childhood homes of Queen Elizabeth, The Queen Mother, who was the youngest daughter of the 14th Earl.

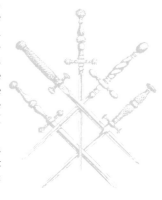

The river that runs near the castle is known as Hermitage Water. Some 600 feet (183m) away from the castle, on the banks of the river, stand the remains of the medieval hermitage which gave Hermitage Castle its name.

HERMITAGE CASTLE
Borders

HERMITAGE, 15 MILES (24 KM) SOUTH OF HAWICK

Great walls of dark sandstone loom menacingly across the Borders, and Sir Walter Scott noted that even in his time the local people regarded this brooding fortress 'with peculiar aversion and terror'.

The merest glance explains why, for the walls rise sheer and imposing from among the grassy earthworks, and windows are few and far between. The only significant openings are the rows of doors on the very top part of the castle, which afforded access to the wooden fighting balcony that once protruded from the walls. The tower was developed from a simple 13th-century rectangular building to the grim fortress that can be seen today, by the Douglas family in the late 14th century.

One of the two great flying arches was reconstructed in the 19th century, but, all in all, Hermitage today appears much as it would have done in the 15th century.

Several of Hermitage's owners committed foul deeds within its walls. One drowned a colleague near the castle, but was later boiled alive for his misdeeds, which included witchcraft. Another starved his enemies to death in the pit dungeons, although he too met an unpleasant end, murdered in a nearby forest. And Hermitage was also where Mary, Queen of Scots rushed to be at the bedside of her ailing lover, the Earl of Bothwell.

Open April to September, daily, and winter weekends. Tel: 0131-244 3101.

Its lonely setting and violent past give Hermitage Castle an eerie atmosphere

HUNTINGTOWER
Tayside

2 MILES (3 KM) WEST OF PERTH

Huntingtower, in Perthshire, was the scene of a famous royal kidnapping

untingtower is one of the most interesting castles in Scotland. It is essentially two towers joined together as one, but intended to be fully independent of each other. The first tower dates from the 15th century and is three storeys tall. In the late 15th or early 16th century, a second rectangular tower was built, a floor higher than the earlier building. In the 17th century, the space between these two towers was walled in and roofed. This remarkable building still displays some original painted ceilings.

One of the most famous events in Scottish history was the 'Raid of Ruthven', which took place at Huntingtower in August 1582. At that time, the castle was called the House of Ruthven and was owned by the powerful Scottish noble, the Earl of Gowrie. The young King James VI was heavily under the influence of two of Gowrie's rivals, the Duke of Lennox and the Earl of Arran. Gowrie and his ally, the Earl of Mar, persuaded the young King to visit the House of Ruthven and then proclaimed him a prisoner. When Arran tried to free the King, he too was imprisoned. Later, Gowrie was executed, and the King ordered that the name of the castle be changed from Ruthven to Huntingtower.

Open all year, daily except winter Fridays and Christmas. Tel: 0131-244 3101.

A story is told that in the 16th century, the daughter of the 1st Earl of Gowrie fell in love with a man whom her family did not consider a suitable match. The young man was given a room in one tower, while the daughter's bedroom was in the other. The daughter had intended to spend the night with her lover, but hearing her mother's footsteps approaching, fled to the roof and leapt from one tower to the other, a span of 9 feet 4 inches (2.8 m). The gap between the two towers is still called the 'Maiden's Leap'.

HUNTLY CASTLE
Grampian

HUNTLY, 12 MILES (19.5 KM) SOUTH-EAST OF KEITH

The once magnificent, palatial castle that is now decayed and crumbling has been described as one of the noblest baronial ruins in Scotland. Approaching the castle along the avenue of trees, you are faced with the vast five-storeyed façade, with its inscriptions, fine oriel windows and handsome carvings. A former Catholic stronghold, Huntly Castle remains an elegant and imposing ruin.

There have been three castles at Huntly. In the 12th century a mound and wooden structure were raised by the Normans, and Robert the Bruce stayed here in 1307, but this building was burned down. In the early 15th century, the Gordons built a second castle, of which only the foundations remain. However, in the 1450s the 4th Earl of Huntly began what he called his 'new werk' and this was basis of the palatial castle that can be seen today. Although it was intended to be an elegant residence, defence was not totally abandoned for comfort. The walls are thick, and there are gun ports and iron gates for added protection.

In 1594 the 5th Earl revolted against King James VI, who then attacked Huntly with gun-powder. Royal favour was lost and won quickly, however; three years later the castle was restored to the Earl, and building resumed. In 1640 Huntly was occupied by the Covenanters.

Open all year, daily except winter Fridays and Christmas. Tel: 0131-244 3101.

Huntly Castle, last rebuilt in 1620, is now an impressive ruin

INNIS CONNEL CASTLE
Strathclyde

LOCH AWE, 18 MILES (29 KM) EAST OF OBAN

The old ruined castle occupies a secure site on Loch Awe

*I*n the 15th century Donald, the infant heir to the Lord of the Isles, was brought to the island fortress of Innis Connel as a prisoner by the Campbell clan. By the time he managed to escape, Donald had reached adulthood. He did not enjoy his freedom for long, for he was recaptured after an ill-conceived invasion of Badenoch in 1503, and was taken to Edinburgh. Poor Donald remained a prisoner at Edinburgh for 40 years.

Innis Connel was an important stronghold of the Campbells of Argyll and was one of their earliest castles. Local tradition suggests that the castle dates from the 11th century, along with the founders of the great

Campbell clan, although there is no architectural evidence that it is so old.

The present building, a squat, square tower, draped in ivy and nestling amid trees, probably dates from the 13th century, and was enlarged in the 15th century. The alterations changed the castle from a simple rectangular tower to a strong enclosure with thick walls following the shape of the island, complete with additional towers. Innis Connel still occupies its little island in Loch Awe, although the view of the castle from the road is somewhat obscured by trees, especially in summer.

The island is privately owned, and there is no public access.

KILCHURN CASTLE
Strathclyde

18 MILES (29 KM) EAST OF OBAN

*I*n an area of reeds and marshes at the northern end of Loch Awe stands Kilchurn Castle, its granite walls and chimneys rising like jagged teeth above the trees. Its position on a peninsula reaching out into the loch gave it some protection from attack on three sides.

The beauty of Kilchurn's setting on this attractive loch has attracted many an artist, but on closer inspection, time has not dealt kindly with the little lakeside fortress and only a shell remains to be seen. Until recently, Kilchurn's unstable walls were a danger to visitors, but these have been secured and the castle may now be viewed from the grounds.

Kilchurn Castle began as a simple square tower with five floors. It was raised in the 15th century by Colin Campbell, 1st Earl of Breadalbane. In the 16th and 17th centuries, the castle was extended. The square tower was incorporated into a small courtyard, with three corner towers, forming an irregular quadrangle. Oddly, the only way into the castle seems to have been through the main door of the keep and across its ground floor. Gun loops placed at regular intervals all around the walls suggest that Kilchurn's builders were more concerned with repelling sudden attacks by Highlanders than in resisting lengthy sieges.

Open access at any reasonable time. Tel: 0131-244 3101.

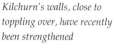

Kilchurn's walls, close to toppling over, have recently been strengthened

KILDRUMMY CASTLE
Grampian

KILDRUMMY, 15 MILES (24 KM) SOUTH OF HUNTLY

Kildrummy, although ruined since 1717, played an important part in Scottish history

Robert the Bruce was married twice. His first wife was a daughter of the powerful Earl of Mar and his second was from the English de Burgh family. Through his first marriage, Robert came into possession of Kildrummy Castle, and it figured prominently in the Scottish wars of independence against Edward I of England.

Like Stirling and Bothwell castles, Kildrummy changed hands several times, most notably after the siege of 1306. Robert's brother, Nigel, had been left in charge of Kildrummy while other supporters of the defeated Bruce hurried north, away from Edward's advancing troops. When Edward laid siege to Kildrummy, Nigel withstood every assault, and his constant counter-attacks made life in the siege camp unbearable. The castle finally fell because of Osbourne, a treacherous blacksmith who was offered gold in return for setting Kildrummy on fire. The garrison surrendered, and Nigel was later executed at Berwick.

Kildrummy Castle today is a seven-sided enclosure with two round towers, two D-shaped towers and a sturdy gatehouse, very much like the one at Harlech. Today, most of this once mighty fortress exists only as foundations in the grass, although some of the towers have survived to first floor level.

Open April to September daily, and winter weekends. Tel: 0131-244 3101.

KYLEAKIN CASTLE
Isle of Skye

KYLEAKIN, OPPOSITE KYLE OF LOCHALSH

S tanding watch over Skye's main harbour, the crumbling walls of Caisteal Maol, or Kyleakin Castle, jab towards the sky like gnarled fingers. These few walls, in a commanding position overlooking the narrow strait between the Isle of Skye and the mainland, are all that remain of a once-powerful MacKinnon fortress that was a vital part of the island's protection against invaders. It was originally a rectangular keep, with walls that were about nine feet (2.7m) thick at the base. The keep was built on a rocky promontory that juts out into the sea, protected by low cliffs on three sides. The fourth side is a slender neck of land that rises only about 20 feet (6.1m) above the high-tide mark.

Little is known of the history of this small fortress, although its architectural style suggests that it dates from the 15th century, and was built on the site of an earlier castle. The keep was probably three storeys high, but the walls no longer stand at their full height.

Legend has it that the Norse owner of the early castle, a woman known as 'Saucy Mary', strung a chain across the entrance of the harbour from the castle to the other side, thus preventing any ships from entering without first paying a toll. When the ships' captains objected, this formidable lady threatened to open fire on them.

Open to access at any reasonable time.

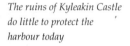
The ruins of Kyleakin Castle do little to protect the harbour today

LINLITHGOW PALACE
Lothian

7 MILES (11.5 KM) SOUTH OF GRANGEMOUTH

One of Scotland's four Royal palaces, Linlithgow was built for James I of Scotland

Rising dramatically from the shores of Linlithgow Loch is a great square palace-fortress, which dates from the 15th century. Although there was a fortified residence here as early as the mid 12th century, and Edward I built a manor here in 1302, it was not until 1425 that work began on the castle that may be seen today.

The Scottish King, James I, gave orders that a royal residence should be constructed on the site of the earlier buildings, and although Linlithgow was primarily a palace, the architect incorporated a number of defensive features. There was a drawbridge and a barbican, and the walls of the four corner towers were immensely thick.

The windows in the lower floors were protected by iron bars, the holes for which can still be seen in the stone. Around the early 1500s, machicolations were added.

Linlithgow has played its part in Scotland's history. Mary, Queen of Scots was born here in 1542, Charles I slept here in 1633 and Cromwell stayed in the Palace in the winter of 1650–51. When the Duke of Cumberland's army bivouacked in Linlithgow in 1746 *en route* to their encounter with Prince Charles Edward Stuart's army at Culloden Moor, fires were left burning which gutted this handsome building.

Open all year, daily except Christmas and New Year. Tel: 0131-244 3101.

LOCH LEVEN CASTLE
Tayside

KINROSS, 10 MILES (16 KM) NORTH OF DUMFERMLINE

Loch Leven Castle is forever associated with the imprisonment of Mary, Queen of Scots

The only way to reach the ancient fortress of Loch Leven is by boat, even though the waters of the loch today are lower than they were in the 14th century when the castle was built. This is because the course of the River Leven was altered in the 19th century, and the level of the loch was lowered as a result. The castle itself is a simple square tower of five storeys, surrounded by a towered wall that was a later addition. The third floor of the tower was possibly where Mary, Queen of Scots was imprisoned between June 1567 and May 1568. There are also the remains of what may have been a private chapel, complete with an altar shelf containing a basin, and a small wall cupboard. IN another window is a closet that may have been used as a strong room in which to store valuables.

Queen Mary was unwell for much of the time she was imprisoned at Loch Leven, and she suffered a miscarriage. She escaped from the castle by befriending the boat keeper, but after the Battle of Langside, during which Mary and her supporters were soundly defeated, she fled the country.

Open from April to September, daily. Tel: 0131-244 3101.

❋
NEIDPATH CASTLE
Borders

JUST WEST OF PEEBLES
❋

The massive tower and turrets of Neidpath Castle rise dramatically from the rock above the River Tweed

*A*fter Scotland had won her independence from England in the 14th century under great warriors like William Wallace and Robert the Bruce, local land-owners had the task of establishing law and order in their domains. Castles such as the one at Neidpath were built, not only to provide a form of defence, should the laird come under attack, but also so that he could maintain a tighter control over his subjects.

Neidpath's L-plan tower was built in the second half of the 14th century, and the upper two floors were re-modelled in the 17th century. The tower is unusual, because both arms of the L form parallelograms, rather than rectangles as was most common, and the corners are rounded. It is an intriguing building, its four main floors intersected with mural passages and 'entresols', or mezzanine floors, giving the impression that the castle is full of small chambers and passages, all at different heights.

The lower floor contained a pit prison and a well, while on the second floor is a room with some fine 17th-century panelling. Mary, Queen of Scots and James I and VI are both known to have stayed at Neidpath, although the castle has been too much altered since the 16th century to be able to identify which rooms they occupied.

Open Easter weekend, then from May to mid October daily. Tel: 01721 720333.

ORCHARDTON TOWER
Dumfries and Galloway

PALNACKIE, 4½ MILES (7 KM) SOUTH OF DALBEATTIE

*O*f all the small tower houses and castles built in 15th century Scotland, Orchardton is one that gives the visitor a clear impression of what domestic life must have been like in Scottish medieval feudal society. The rooms inside the tower are small, cramped and dark, with narrow windows, which perhaps would have made for warmer living quarters – they certainly would have made the tower more secure from attack. But during winter, with the shutters firmly closed against the cold and a smoking fire in the hearth, Orchardton Castle would not have been a cheerful dwelling.

Orchardton is unusual because it is the only round tower house in Scotland. It was built in the mid 15th century by the Provost of Lincluden.

The basement had a vaulted roof, and unlike the other floors, is rectangular. The narrow spiral staircase is in the thickness of the wall, and rises to the top of the 33-foot (10m) high tower, where there is a gabled watchtower. Like Norman keeps, the entrance was on the first floor, so that the wooden steps which gave access to the tower could be drawn up inside the building during times of danger.

Open access at all reasonable times. Tel: 0131-244 3101.

Built by John Cairns, Orchardton Tower is the only circular tower house left standing in Scotland

ST ANDREWS CASTLE
Fife

ST ANDREWS, 13 MILES (21 KM) SOUTH-EAST OF DUNDEE

The jagged ruins of St Andrews Castle cling to a low grassy cliff on the coast

*I*n March 1546 the Protestant preacher George Wishart was burned in front of the walls of St Andrews Castle by the ambitious Archbishop of St Andrews, Cardinal David Beaton. Beaton was not a popular man, chiefly because he refused to agree to the marriage of Henry VIII's Protestant son to the Scottish king's Catholic daughter. Later that year, a group of Protestant Fife lairds gained access to the castle and murdered Beaton, hanging his body from the castle walls in a pair of sheets. Following this, a long siege began, as the forces of the Regent of Scotland tried to oust them from the castle.

It was during this turbulent time that the famous mine and counter-mine were dug. The attackers' mine was intended to go under the foundations, so that the wall would weaken, while the counter-mine attempted to stop it. You can still walk through these two tunnels, which give a unique insight into medieval warfare.

This ancient castle was built and used by the Bishops and Archbishops of St Andrews. It comprises a five-sided enclosure, protected on two sides by the sea, with buildings dating from the 12th to the 16th centuries that served as palace, fortress, and prison.

Open all year daily, except Christmas and New Year. Tel: 0131-244 3101.

One of the castle's most famous features is its sinister bottle dungeon. This is a pit 24 feet (7.3m) deep, which is narrow at the top and wider at the bottom – much like the shape of a bottle. Once you are inside, you cannot scale the walls to escape. Hewn out of solid rock, it has no windows or openings for air.

CASTLE STALKER
Strathclyde

18 MILES (29 KM) NORTH OF OBAN

*S*tanding on a tiny island in Loch Laich, this small tower house can be seen from the road that runs from Ballachulish towards Oban. It bears some resemblance to the castle of Eilean Donan, since both are set in lonely sites, surrounded by water, and are simple tower structures.

Historically, it would appear that access to Castle Stalker has always been by boat, and no causeway has ever been built to make it more easily accessible, but at low tide it is possible to wade across the shallow waters of the loch.

The castle itself is a rectangular tower, about 45 feet (14m) by 36 feet (11m) at its base, and was built in the 16th century. The fact that its walls were nine feet (2.7m) thick, coupled with the inaccessibility of its site, meant that it was fairly well protected against would-be invaders. The entrance was at first floor level, and access originally would have been up wooden steps, or a ladder that could have been drawn up into the tower in times of danger. The stone stairway that can be seen today was a later addition.

Castle Stalker became derelict after the Second Jacobite Rising in the 18th century, and was restored only recently.

The castle is not open to the public, but clearly visible from the main road.

Cut off from the land, Castle Stalker's defences were effective throughout its history

STIRLING CASTLE
Central

STIRLING, 22 MILES (35.5 KM) WEST OF DUNFERMLINE

Set on a high rock, Stirling Castle has played a major role in Scotland's history

Perched high and proud on its towering cliffs, Stirling Castle is a complex arrangement of buildings, some plain and functional, others splendid and palatial, that reflect its long history as one of the most important castles in Scotland.

Most of the buildings that can be seen today date from the 15th century or later, and it is not known exactly what the castle was like before this, when it was being fought over by William Wallace, Robert the Bruce and Edward I. This eventful history began in the late 11th century, when a wooden structure was raised. Edward I seized Stirling in 1296 and Wallace took it back in 1297. He lost it again in 1298, but the Scots reclaimed it once more in 1299. Edward retrieved the castle after a furious siege in 1304, and this time held it until the English defeat at Bannockburn in 1314.

There are many fine buildings to explore in this splendid fortress. Perhaps the most impressive is the Great Hall, which is one of the earliest Renaissance buildings in Scotland. The elegant Palace was built for James V in the 1540s, and there are some exquisite carvings, both inside (around the fireplaces) and on the exterior walls.

Open all year daily. Tel: 0131-244 3101.

Below and right,Tantallon, with its towering red sandstone walls poised on the edge of the cliffs, is a spectacular sight

TANTALLON CASTLE
Lothian

2½ MILES (4 KM) EAST OF NORTH BERWICK

To enable Tantallon to withstand sieges, arrangements were made for the castle to take in supplies from the seaward side. The remains of a crane bastion can be seen, where provisions were winched from boats anchored below, and it is likely that there was another one in the now ruined sea gate.

The great red walls of Tantallon Castle form one of the strongest and most daunting castles in Scotland. Perched on a spur of rock, with sheer cliffs plummeting into frothing seas on three of its sides, the fourth side is protected by a formidable array of ditches and walls. Rising from one of the three great gaping ditches, and sweeping clear across the neck of the promontory, is a vast curtain of red sandstone. This wall is 12 feet (3.7m) thick, and a staggering 50 feet (15m) tall. Although cannons and storms have battered this mighty wall, it remains one of the most impressive defensive features of any castle in Britain.

Tantallon is associated with one of Scotland's most famous families – the Red Douglases, Earls of Angus. It came into their hands at the end of the 14th century, and became their base as they plotted and fought against their enemies. But it was not until 1528 that the mighty fortress of Tantallon was seriously put to the test, when King James V himself laid siege to the Red Douglas stronghold.

Sixteenth-century Scottish politics were complicated, but, essentially, Archibald Douglas, 6th Earl of Angus, had kept the young James V a virtual prisoner in Edinburgh during his minority. James finally managed to escape, and once he was old enough to act for himself, he charged Douglas with treason. James brought a great battery of guns from Dunbar Castle, and for 20 days pounded the walls of Tantallon with everything he had. Tantallon, however, stood firm – perhaps because the great ditches to the front of the castle prevented the guns from being brought too close, and perhaps because the king ran short of powder and shot. The castle eventually fell to James, but as a result of negotiations rather than firepower. Douglas fled the country, and James began work to reinforce and repair Tantallon's medieval defences. After the King's death, Douglas returned from exile in 1543 and immediately began plotting against the Regent of Scotland, the Earl of Arran.

The ruins at Tantallon are impressive and the Mid Tower, which has been changed and developed through the centuries, stands almost complete. It was originally five storeys, but suffered during the 1528 siege. In 1556, a Fore Tower was added, designed both to withstand and to house cannon. The East Tower was also five storeys, and there are still stairs in the massive curtain wall that lead to the battlements.

Open April to September daily, and most days in winter. Tel: 0131-244 3101.

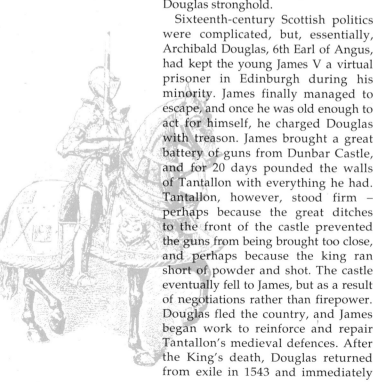

Although William Forbes was not a figure of national significance, he was well respected locally. Generous to local people, by all accounts he was unusually cultured and enlightened for a laird of his time.

TOLQUHON CASTLE
Grampian

PITMEDDEN, 15 MILES (24 KM) NORTH OF ABERDEEN

'*A*l this warke excep the auld tour was begun be William Forbes 15 Aprile 1584 and endit be him 20 October 1589. '

These words are inscribed in a panel high up on the right hand side of the imposing gatehouse at Tolquhon Castle (pronounced 'Tuh-hon'). They refer to the work of the 7th Lord of Tolquhon, the cultured William Forbes, who inherited the castle in the late 16th century. Before Tolquhon came into

Forbes' possession, it was little more than a single tower (the 'auld tour') with some adjoining walls. But in 1584, Forbes decided the tower was insufficient for his needs, and set about extending it. The result was the fine palatial building that can be visited today, and although Tolquhon is now a ruin, it takes little imagination to envisage how splendid this castle must have looked in its heyday.

The 'auld tour', or Preston's Tower,

Right, now a roofless ruin, Tolquhon remains an impressive and handsome castle

was raised in the early 15th century, probably by John Preston, its namesake. It was built of granite, with thick walls, and had small rooms which would have been ill-lit and probably cramped for the people living in them. Little remains of Preston's Tower except the vaulted basement and parts of the first floor. Forbes used it as one of the corners of his new castle, and extended the building to make a four-sided structure around a large courtyard. The castle was entered through a gatehouse which, although it appears to be formidable with its gun loops and round towers, had thin walls and would not have withstood a serious attack. It was designed for show, rather than defence.

An impressive array of buildings line all four sides of the fine cobbled courtyard. To the east are the kitchens and an unpleasant pit-prison, while the main house is to the south. This building contained the hall – a spacious, airy room lit by large windows, and the laird's personal chambers, along with additional bed chambers and a gallery. Contemporary records show that William Forbes owned many books, and it is likely that they would have been displayed here.

Forbes' work here did not stop with his fine new house, but extended to the grounds. The hall and his private chamber looked out over a formal garden, and though this has long since disappeared, the remains of a dovecote and recesses for bees have been discovered in the walls.

Open from April to September, daily; weekends only in winter. Tel: 0131-244 3101.

Above and right, Urquhart is a famous landmark on the shores of Loch Ness

❖
URQUHART CASTLE
Highland

DRUMNADROCHIT, 16 MILES (26 KM) SOUTH-WEST OF INVERNESS

❖

*I*n 1545 the fearsome Macdonald clan swept into the quiet Glen of Urquhart, looting and pillaging as they went. They laid siege to the castle and plundered it mercilessly, taking chairs, tables, gates, armour, food and even the pillows from the beds. After the castle had been thoroughly sacked, the raiders turned their attention to the homesteads in the valley. This was just one incident in a long history of warfare and bloodshed that had raged since a castle was first built on the

shores of Loch Ness in the early 13th century. The first recorded owner of the castle was Alan Durward, Lord of Atholl. Durward's brother-in-law was Alexander II, King of Scotland, and it would seem that the young king was very much under the influence of his powerful relative.

In 1296 Edward I of England seized Urquhart along with other castles in the area, but his hold was precarious and he lost it again by 1303. Edward marched north and retook the castle,

but within five years Robert the Bruce had attacked Edward's garrison and secured Urquhart for himself.

Although Urquhart remained in the hands of the Scottish government during the 14th and 15th centuries, it was not an easy ownership. Not only was the castle under threat from the English, but there was a constant threat of attack from the Lords of the Isles. These fiercely independent people had been forced into the Kingdom of Scotland after the Battle of Largs in 1263, and were so keen to regain their freedom that they even sided with the English. Urquhart passed from the Lords of the Isles to the Scottish government and back again in a long series of bloody encounters that continued until the Lordship of the Isles no longer existed.

In view of its turbulent history, it is not surprising that Urquhart's defences are formidable. A walled causeway, with a drawbridge halfway along, led to the castle gatehouse. Great walls that followed the contours of the rock protected it from attack, strengthened by a ditch at the front and the loch at the back. Inside the walls were a variety of buildings, including living quarters, a chapel, kitchens and a dove-cote. Although much is ruined, apart from the 16th century tower house which is still largely intact, this romantic ruin huddled on the loch shore is well worth a visit.

Open all year daily, except Christmas and January. Tel: 0131-244 3101.

Looking for the Monster
Visitors to Loch Ness may be more familiar with the tales of the monster than with Urquhart Castle. 'Nessie' first made an appearance to a monk in the 8th century, and many hundreds of people have claimed to have seen it since, especially during the last 100 years or so. Eye-witness accounts do not readily agree – it has variously been described as a coiled serpent and as a great crocodile.

INDEX